WALKING THE TOUR OF THE LAKE DISTRICT

A NINE-DAY CIRCUIT OF CUMBRIA'S FELLS, VALLEYS AND LAKES

by Lesley Williams

CICERONE

JUNIPER HOUSE, MURLEY MOSS,
OXENHOLME ROAD, KENDAL, CUMBRIA LA9 7RL
www.cicerone.co.uk

© Lesley Williams 2021
Second edition 2021
ISBN: 978 1 78631 049 1
First edition 2007

Printed in China on responsibly sourced paper on behalf of Latitude Press Ltd
A catalogue record for this book is available from the British Library.
All photographs are by the author unless otherwise stated.

© Crown copyright 2021 OS PU100012932

Updates to this Guide

While every effort is made by our authors to ensure the accuracy of guidebooks as they go to print, changes can occur during the lifetime of an edition. This guidebook was researched and written before and during the COVID-19 pandemic. While we are not aware of any significant changes to routes or facilities at the time of printing, it is likely that the pandemic will give rise to more changes than would usually be expected. Any updates that we know of for this guide will be on the Cicerone website (www.cicerone.co.uk/1049/updates), so please check before planning your trip. We also advise that you check information about such things as transport, accommodation and shops locally. Even rights of way can be altered over time.

We are always grateful for information about any discrepancies between a guidebook and the facts on the ground, sent by email to updates@cicerone.co.uk or by post to Cicerone, Juniper House, Murley Moss, Oxenholme Road, Kendal, LA9 7RL.

Register your book: To sign up to receive free updates, special offers and GPX files where available, register your book at www.cicerone.co.uk.

Front cover: The descent to Buttermere (Stage 4)

CONTENTS

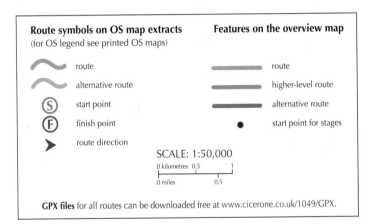

Route symbols on OS map extracts
(for OS legend see printed OS maps)

~ route

~ alternative route

(S) start point

(F) finish point

➤ route direction

Features on the overview map

━━━ route

━━━ higher-level route

━━━ alternative route

● start point for stages

SCALE: 1:50,000

0 kilometres 0.5   1

0 miles   0.5

GPX files for all routes can be downloaded free at www.cicerone.co.uk/1049/GPX.

Mountain safety

Every mountain walk has its dangers, and those described in this guidebook are no exception. All who walk or climb in the mountains should recognise this and take responsibility for themselves and their companions along the way. The author and publisher have made every effort to ensure that the information contained in this guide was correct when it went to press, but, except for any liability that cannot be excluded by law, they cannot accept responsibility for any loss, injury or inconvenience sustained by any person using this book.

International distress signal *(emergency only)*
Six blasts on a whistle (and flashes with a torch after dark) spaced evenly for one minute, followed by a minute's pause. Repeat until an answer is received. The response is three signals per minute followed by a minute's pause.

Helicopter rescue
The following signals are used to communicate with a helicopter:

Help needed:
raise both arms
above head to
form a 'Y'

Help not needed:
raise one arm
above head, extend
other arm downward

Emergency telephone numbers
Dial 999 or 112 and ask for 'Cumbria Police' then 'Mountain Rescue'
For the emergency SMS service, text 999 and send 'Police' + details of incident + location

Weather reports
www.lakedistrictweatherline.co.uk
www.metoffice.gov.uk
www.mwis.org.uk

ROUTE SUMMARY TABLE

Stage	Start	Distance	Ascent	Descent	Time	Page
Prologue	Windermere	10.5km (6½ miles)	350m	400m	2hr 45min	32
Stage 1	Ambleside	20km (12½ miles)	610m	610m	6hr	36
Stage 2	Coniston	18km (11 miles)	865m	855m	6hr–6hr 30min	44
Stage 2A	Coniston	22km (13¾ miles)	1200m	1190m	8hr	52
Stage 3	Eskdale	18km (11 miles) or 20km (12½ miles)	470m	460m	5hr–5hr 30min or 6–6hr 30min	61
Stage 3A	Eskdale	17km (10½ miles)	980m	970m	6hr 30min	68
Stage 4	Wasdale Head	12km (7½ miles)	780m	750m	4hr 30min–5hr	74
Stage 4A	Wasdale Head	16.5km (10 miles)	1150m	1110m	6hr 30min	79
Stage 5	Buttermere	16km (10 miles)	490m	515m	5hr	86
Stage 5A	Buttermere	17.5km (11 miles)	1020m	1050m	7hr	92
Stage 6	Keswick	15.5km (9½ miles)	560m	560m	5hr	100
Stage 7	Rosthwaite	14km (8 miles)	580m	600m	5hr	107
Stage 8	Grasmere	13km (8 miles)	610m	530m	4hr	113
Stage 8A	Grasmere	16km (10 miles) or 19.5km (12 miles)	1100m	1020m	6hr or 6hr 30min	119
Stage 9	Patterdale	18km (11 miles) or 15km (9½ miles)	750m	840m	5–6hr or 4hr 15min	127
Total (main route, excluding prologue)		**144.5km (90 miles)**	**5720m**	**5720m**	**9 days**	
Total (using high-level alternatives)		**156.5km (97 miles)**	**7950m**	**7950m**	**9–10 days**	

Alternative schedules

*B = Buttermere *WH = Wasdale Head

Kms from Ambleside		Kms from Ambleside	13 days plus prologue	9 days plus prologue	7 days plus prologue
Windermere ►	10	10.5	Prologue *10.5km 2hr 45min*	Prologue *10.5km 2hr 45min*	Prologue *10.5km 2hr 45min*
	5				
Ambleside ►	0				
Elterwater ►	5	8.8	Ambleside to Elterwater *8.8km 2hr 30min*	Ambleside to Coniston *20km 6hr*	Ambleside to Coniston *20km 6hr*
	10				
	15	20	Elterwater to Coniston *11.2km 3hr 30min*		
Coniston ►	20				
	25	29	Coniston to Seathwaite *9km 3hr 15min*	Coniston to Eskdale *18km 6hr–6hr 30min*	Coniston to Eskdale *18km 6hr–6hr 30min*
Seathwaite ► (camping)	30				
	35	38	Seathwaite to Eskdale *9km 2hr 45min– 3hr 15min*		
Doctor Bridge, ► Eskdale	40				
	45	(48.7)	Eskdale to Nether Wasdale *10.7km 3hr 20min*	Eskdale to Wasdale Head *18km 5hr–5hr 30min*	Eskdale to Black Sail *24km 7hr 45min*
Nether Wasdale ►	50				
	55	56	Nether Wasdale to Wasdale Head *9.3km 2hr 10min*		
Wasdale Head ►	55				
	60	62	WH to Black Sail *6km 2hr 45min*	Wasdale Head to Buttermere *12km 4hr 30min–5hr*	
Black Sail ►	65	68	Black Sail to B *6km 2hr*		Black Sail to Keswick *22km 7hr*
Buttermere ►					
	70				
	75	84	Buttermere to Keswick *16km 5hr*	Buttermere to Keswick *16km 5hr*	
	80				
Keswick ►	85				
	90	99.5	Keswick to Rosthwaite *15.5km 5hr*	Keswick to Rosthwaite *15.5km 5hr*	Keswick to Rosthwaite *15.5km 5hr*
	95				
Rosthwaite ►	100				
	105	113.5	Rosthwaite to Grasmere *14km 5hr*	Rosthwaite to Grasmere *14km 5hr*	Rosthwaite to Patterdale *27km 9hr*
	110				
Grasmere ►	115				
	120	126.5	Grasmere to Patterdale *13km 4hr*	Grasmere to Patterdale *13km 4hr*	
	125				
Patterdale ►	130				
	135	144.5	Patterdale to Ambleside *18km 5–6hr*	Patterdale to Ambleside *18km 5–6hr*	Patterdale to Ambleside *18km 5–6hr*
	140				
Ambleside ►	145				

Acknowledgements

The concept of a circular trek around the Lake District was first thought of by Jim Reid while working as a local youth hostel warden. Jim spent two happy years researching and writing the first Tour of the Lake District guidebook which was published by Cicerone in 2007. With other commitments filling his life, his original book was in need of a fresh approach. The basic framework for the lower-level main route remains similar for most of the stages, any alterations reflecting changes in the quality of the paths, access or signage on the ground. The stage between Keswick and Rosthwaite now runs to the east of Derwent Water, enjoying fine views and a visit to Castlerigg Stone Circle, and the final stage from Patterdale now returns directly via Scandale to finish in Ambleside.

I am deeply grateful for the help and support of my husband Jonathan, who has accompanied me on many of my research walks, including undertaking many of the higher summit alternative routes while I walked or re-walked the lower route. His help and support also extended to helping me organise the mass of information collected, and patiently listening to my accounts of lone wanderings on the fells during some of the challenging stormy days of the winter of 2019–20.

Finally, my thanks to the team at Cicerone, for ensuring that I have enjoyed all the help, guidance and support afforded to all our authors, despite being an 'in-house' author!

PREFACE

A perfect winter morning for photography – Elter Water

'I wandered lonely as a cloud
that floats on high o'er vales and hills,
and all at once I saw a crowd
a host, of golden daffodils'
William Wordsworth

Like many English schoolchildren, I learnt Wordsworth's poem, inspired by the Lake District's scenery, by heart – but it wasn't until my first visit on a walking holiday as a teenager that I fell in love with the Lakes. It was a typical week of 'summer' weather: warm and humid one minute, interspersed with driving wind and torrential rain giving rise to swollen streams and boggy ground ready to seemingly swallow you whole. But for the first time I understood that the colours, the views and the unspoilt wildness was everything I needed to make me happy. The freedom of the mind and body as you wander among the Lake District fells and valleys is something to be experienced and cherished at any age, and in my research for this book, whether walking alone or in company, I have genuinely enjoyed every minute – whatever the weather!

However you choose to use this book, whether for a series of long weekends, or for an adventurous high mountain expedition, I hope you enjoy your experiences as much as I have enjoyed discovering new paths and views while researching this book.

Looking west from just below the summit of Whiteless Pike, with Rannerdale Knotts and Crummock Water below (Stage 5A)

INTRODUCTION

Still waters on Buttermere provide stunning reflections (Stage 4)

The Lake District National Park is one of England's most popular mountain regions, designated as a UNESCO World Heritage site, welcoming millions of visitors every year. For fell walkers, experiencing the beauty of the mountains and lakes happens at a relatively slow pace, giving time to admire all that the national park has to offer, away from the crowds that throng the valleys and lakesides. Whether you are an experienced fell walker or are considering your first visit, the Tour of the Lake District will reveal many rewarding views and memorable experiences – the best of the Lake District in a circular tour.

The Lake District is the name given to the mountains and lakes of Cumbria, a region of north-west England that forms a roughly circular bulge in the coastline before the border with Scotland is reached near Carlisle. It's a region that has been settled by man from ancient times. Neolithic stone circles, the distinctive local Celtic and Norse names, ancient packhorse bridges, castles and medieval farmsteads, quarries and the open fells themselves all bear testament to the fascinating history and landscape that can be explored while walking this multi-day route.

In just one day you can experience a cross section of history and landscape. One bright winter day I explored a new route to Rosthwaite from Keswick. A steady climb brought me first to the atmospheric setting of the world-renowned stone circle at Castlerigg, then on through farmland and sunken tracks to Walla Crag to take in the extensive views of the northern and western fells, and a bird's-eye view of two lakes – one natural, one man-made. I crossed several ancient packhorse bridges, literally no wider than a horse, passed through the dappled light of the oak and ash woodlands of Ashness, and into the 'hidden' valley of Watendlath, at the head of which lies a small lake and one of the more remote hamlets in the entire region, the pastures still grazed by Herdwick sheep whose ancestors grazed these same slopes centuries ago. A final climb over open grassy fells brought me down to Rosthwaite in Borrowdale, the Norse name meaning 'The clearing with a cairn'. This village lies at the junction of three great valleys surrounding the Borrowdale fells, now a stage point for walkers on the Coast to Coast walk, the Cumbria Way and the Tour of the Lake District.

It's perhaps astonishing that the idea of a circular walking route taking in the best of the Lake District is just that – an idea, with no fixed route, and no signposts of any kind. This guide can be followed exactly, or it can be used as the basis for your own route around the Lake District.

The route described takes in most of the major valleys of the region, staying away from many of the tourist honeypots near Windermere, preferring to explore ancient routes that link one valley with the next, one village with another. There are both high-level and lower-level options described for some stages; the high-level routes start and finish at the same points as the lower-level options, so it's easy to mix and match as you go, according to weather conditions, energy and time available.

LANDSCAPE AND GEOLOGY

A quick glance at a map of the Lake District suggests two obvious things: that it is a mountainous area, and that it is interspersed by a network of long thin 'finger lakes' which spread in a radial formation from roughly the centre of the region. But this is a complex landscape. The geology of the region is roughly divided into three broad zones. In the north, the most ancient rocks of the region are the Skiddaw slates, today forming the bulky rounded fells to the north of Keswick. In the middle are steeper, craggy mountains made of much harder volcanic material, while to the south and forming a rim around the edge of the Lake District are lower, undulating hills made up mainly of sedimentary rocks.

The origin of the Skiddaw slates dates back to when the area formed a tiny part of a tectonic plate that lay south of the equator, submerged in

Penny Hill Farm nestles in Eskdale (Stage 2)

a shallow sea. Mud, sand and silts were deposited, but around 475 million years ago these deposits were subjected to immense heat and pressure as the plate on which the 'Lake District' lay began to move north, colliding with neighbouring continental plates. The resulting changes from muds to rock led to the formation of incredibly hard slates of the Ordovician Skiddaw Group.

Around 460 million years ago continued movement of the continental plates caused violent volcanic activity, with layer upon layer of molten lavas of various viscosity and ash building up to form a central core to the region, characterised by the steep crags seen surrounding Thirlmere, High Rigg, Walla Crag, Kirk Fell and on into Wasdale and Eskdale. These volcanic rocks are also threaded with rich veins of minerals,

the result of highly mineral-rich liquids and gases which penetrated tiny fissures within the rock.

Over the next 400 million years the region continued to move north, crossing the equator and undergoing a series of periods of erosion and deposition both above and below the sea to form limestones, sands, and even coal deposits. Many more periods of deposition and tectonic activity repeatedly squashed and buckled the region to form a dome. This shape led to the formation of a radial drainage system as rivers carried away the softer sedimentary rocks, exposing the underlying older Skiddaw and Borrowdale rocks, leaving just a fringe of the sedimentary deposits.

Finally, two and a half million years ago, along with much of northern England and Scotland, the region was covered in a huge ice sheet up to

700m thick in places. Glaciers carved into the established radial drainage system, forming deep U-shaped valleys such as Langdale and Patterdale, in-between which lie craggy crests and ridges – fine examples being Sharp Edge and Striding Edge. Other glacial and periglacial features include isolated rocks or 'glacial erratics', and the finger lakes seen today. Many of these lakes are incredibly deep, while others have been modified – Crummock Water and Buttermere formed when one huge lake was split by the accumulation of silt and deposits draining in from the fells and rivers to the north and south.

Over the years the rich mineral resources of the region have been exploited by man, scarring the landscape. The Romans were first to begin lead mining, but over the years slate and copper mining was a major industry, especially in the area around Coniston, while rarer deposits such as graphite and tungsten have been found and exploited in other valleys and fells and especially in the mineral-rich Caldbeck fells to the north.

PLANTS AND WILDLIFE

Prior to the 1600s, ancient woodland would have covered much of the valleys and hillsides – although tree felling in the area dates from Neolithic times when axes were first fashioned and used. This ancient woodland has now all but disappeared due to further clearing for grazing, and the practice of coppicing for the charcoal industry. Today, the most common woodlands

An ancient oak tree in Wasdale (Stage 3)

are made up of a mixture of oak, ash, birch, hazel and holly, planted between the 17th and 19th centuries for the coppice and charcoal industries, while on higher ground larch and spruce plantations can be found.

The meadows and grasslands in the valleys form a patchwork of colour through the seasons, with wildflowers including wild daffodils and bluebells flourishing in lightly wooded areas and in meadows that have been allowed to remain free from artificial fertilisers. Meanwhile the rough grazing dotted with bracken, juniper, bilberries and heather found on the lower slopes of the fells is home to flocks of Herdwick sheep, an ancient hardy breed well adapted to life in these parts. The high fells can be both rocky and boggy, and both types of terrain will be experienced while following the route in this book. The plant life within these uppermost regions consists of bog-loving species such as sphagnum mosses and cotton grass, while rocky outcrops hide tiny alpine plants and lichens.

The larger wild animals of the Lake District include roe deer and red deer, badgers and foxes, and in some areas otters have been seen. Smaller mammals include rabbits and hares, as well as the red squirrel which flourishes in carefully managed woodlands where its larger grey cousin is actively discouraged.

Birdlife is diverse. The high fells have been the home of golden eagles; however, sadly the last remaining male can no longer be seen riding the thermals. Ospreys continue to thrive and return each year to their nesting sites near Bassenthwaite, while buzzards, ravens and peregrine falcons also patrol the skies, along with curlews, skylarks and many other bird species.

The countryside and fells are teeming with insects during the summer months, but besides the possibility of being on the receiving end of a bite from a hungry mosquito, there is nothing for the walker to fear. Wasps and bees generally keep to the tourist areas in the valleys, but a little care should be taken on the lower slopes on hot summer days as adders can very occasionally be found basking in the sunshine. However, they will only bite if they are picked up or threatened in some way.

The Lake District has a high population of ticks, which is at its peak during late spring and early summer. Humans are most at risk of picking up ticks when brushing through tall vegetation, especially bracken. Most of the route described in this guide will tend to be on open fell hillside, with a minimal risk; however, some sections may be more overgrown, particularly in mid to late summer. To minimise risk of being bitten, apply insect repellent and cover skin, especially legs and arms, with lightweight clothing. To remove a tick, use tick tweezers and follow the instructions. If symptoms of Lyme disease occur – such as headaches and muscle aches – seek medical assistance. For more information see www.lymediseaseaction.org.uk.

FARMING

The landscape seen today across the Lake District has evolved over many centuries. The drystone walls forming the field systems of the valley bottoms, as well as the 'intake' and 'outgang' divisions of the lower slopes, provide today's hill farmers with tried and tested enclosures for managing the movement and grazing of livestock. It is these 'special qualities' of the landscape that are inscribed in recognition as a World Heritage site. Farming, along with tourism, is a core part of the Lake District economy, and maintaining the unique look of the land while developing modern and sustainable practices is an important new challenge in this often hostile environment.

The ancient native breed of Herdwick sheep are hardy animals well adapted to the climate and rugged hillsides. The word 'herdwyck' means sheep pasture. The lambs are generally born black, their fleeces gradually lightening to the more characteristic grey as they get older. The Herdwick flocks are hefted, spending much of their lives on common open fellsides – especially in the Duddon Valley – without the need for shepherding or enclosure. Hefting becomes a learned behaviour, passed from ewe to lamb over succeeding generations. Lambs graze with their mothers on the 'heaf' (land) belonging to their farm and build an intimate knowledge of where the best grazing and shelter can be found.

Other breeds of sheep you may see include the popular Swaledale – a hardy medium-sized breed, characterised by their black faces and horns, with bright white around their noses and eyes; Rough Fell sheep are similar but larger and more docile, with black faces except for a white patch on the

Herdwick sheep in the Duddon Valley moving to a new lower pasture in winter

nose, and a long, coarse fleece; and Cheviots are white-faced and hornless, and tend to be more alert and active.

Lambing generally takes place any time between February and May; at these times, and while the ewes are pregnant, it's particularly important to keep dogs under close supervision.

Cows are grazed for milk and meat products, the meat being some of the best quality in the country – and there are also some excellent local cheeses to taste. Traditional agricultural shows and sheep dog trails take place throughout the region between May and September.

HISTORY AND CULTURE

Man first entered the area probably around 7500 years ago, in the Middle Stone Age. Archaeological evidence from early settlements around 6000 years ago comes in the form of stone circles and standing stones, and in the stone axes and cup- and ring-marked rocks in Great Langdale. Stone axes from Pike of Stickle – the main site for the Langdale Neolithic axe factory – were roughly cut into shape and then sent to coastal communities to be finished and polished for trading throughout the country. Bronze Age culture followed, with the clearing of trees and rocks in the valleys to form fields for livestock, outlined by drystone walls.

Later the Celts arrived (although some historians suggest that the Celts may have been indigenous to the area), giving rise to the name Cumbria, the modern name for the county derived from Cumberland, meaning 'Cumbra Land' – land of the Cymry. The Romans further exerted influence on the land, adding an infrastructure of roads, towns and fortresses including roads between Ambleside (home to a fort named Galava) and Ravenglass via Hardknott Fort and High Street, a broad ridge route between Ambleside and Penrith climbing to around 700m.

After the fall of the Roman Empire the Celtic people of the region continued farming, but from AD600 the Anglo-Saxons began to spread into the region, and most Cumbric/Celtic names and language died out. The Norse invaders between AD700 and AD1000 made further clearings of forest and scrublands to graze cattle and sheep higher in the mountains and built more extensive networks of the drystone walls that define many field boundaries to this day.

Throughout the following 600 years the region was subjected to waves of conflict and rivalry, but also saw a gradual increase in prosperity. By the 18th century the area had begun to be recognised for its beauty, aided by the early writings of Thomas Gray in 1769. Later, an increasing number of tourists with an appreciation of wild and natural beauty arrived using the developing railways and transport system. William Wordsworth's book *A Guide*

Through the District of the Lakes was published in many editions during the early 1830s, and at the time outsold his poetry. It became one of the first books to encourage an appreciation of scenery as a whole. Artists and writers flocked to visit and settle in the area, including John Ruskin, Samuel Taylor Coleridge, Harriet Martineau and JMW Turner, and with them came the tourists, further encouraged by the writings of Beatrix Potter and Arthur Ransome in more recent times.

Today visitors come to enjoy the lakes and views, with all the trappings of the modern tourist industry at their disposal. However, to fully appreciate this wonderful and unique area it is far better to travel more slowly and with care, walking the ancient paths and routes through the valleys and fells. This way you are able to be more mindful of the landscape and ecology as you immerse yourself in your surroundings, enjoy hard-won views, and give back to the local communities whose ancestors once took pioneering steps to tame this wild and beautiful place.

THE TOUR OF THE LAKE DISTRICT

The main route described is for a circular tour that will take between one and two weeks to complete. The route is presented in nine stages and generally uses lower, easier paths and tracks linking most of the main valleys. It is suitable for most walkers, including active families with older children able to walk for sometimes up to five or six hours each day. The Tour can be fitted into a week by either combining some of the shorter stages or by taking public transport alternatives, or

The Moot Hall stands in the centre of the Market Square in Keswick (Stages 5, 5A and 6)

Walkers enjoying superb winter walking between Walla Crag and Ashness (Stage 6)

you can take your time and extend the Tour over two weeks, giving scope to visit many attractions on the way. Also described are a series of alternative routes that will take you to some of the Lake District's highest fells, including Coniston Old Man, Scafell Pike, Great Gable and Helvellyn. Extending the route with higher alternatives is ideal for fit and experienced walkers and those with more time available when the weather is settled.

There is no need to bring a car as the route begins with a 'prologue' stage to Ambleside from the train terminus station at Windermere. If you prefer to make your way directly to Ambleside, it is just a ten-minute bus ride, or a short ride on the lake steamer.

The prologue begins at Windermere rail station and leaves the town quickly to gain the first of many fantastic viewpoints along the way at Orrest Head. From here an undulating route crosses farmland and meadows, passing the historic farmstead of Townend and continuing on an ancient track to Ambleside.

Ambleside is a popular centre for walkers and outdoor enthusiasts, providing an opportunity to pick up any items you feel you need or have forgotten. Leaving the town, height is gained as Loughrigg Tarn is passed, then a beautiful riverside walk leads to the village of Elterwater nestling in the Great Langdale valley. Another climb follows to gain access to Little Langdale, and later the route passes picturesque Tarn Hows before arriving in the busy village of Coniston with its good range of facilities.

From Coniston there are low- and high-level route alternatives, both passing over the Coniston fells to

19

reach the beautiful Duddon Valley, then onwards either directly or via Hardknott Roman Fort to Eskdale, one of the more remote and beautiful valleys in the western Lake District.

After an enjoyable riverside walk through Upper Eskdale you can choose from a high- or low-level route to either climb England's highest mountain, Scafell Pike, or ascend more easily through woodland before dropping into Wasdale, where accommodation is available either at Nether Wasdale or at Wasdale Head at the far end of West Water, England's deepest lake and voted Britain's favourite view.

From Wasdale Head, further choices present themselves. The iconic Great Gable can be summited before making a traverse across the flank of Brandreth and over Hay Stacks and then descending to Buttermere; or a slightly easier route ascends to Black Sail Pass, passes by the tiny Black Sail Youth Hostel at the head of Ennerdale, then climbs again to gain views from Scarth Gap down into the beautiful broad Buttermere valley.

The route to Keswick also has a choice of high- and lower-level options. A stunning ridge walk via Whiteless Pike, Crag Hill and Causey Pike is one for a fine clear day; alternatively, a lower route climbs through the Derwent fells before descending to Derwent Water and on to Keswick – which, like Ambleside, is a popular centre for walkers and all outdoor activities.

From Keswick the Tour ascends to the atmospheric Castlerigg Stone Circle, then on to Walla Crag for fine views. It continues through woods to the hidden valley of Watendlath before reaching the village of Rosthwaite in the Borrowdale valley.

The stage from Rosthwaite climbs over the wild fells of Greenup Edge, with boggy ground to cross, before descending to Grasmere. This is a relatively short stage, giving ample time to visit Dove Cottage and the Wordsworth museum.

From Grasmere you can either climb to the summit of Helvellyn and drop from there to Patterdale, or you can take a lower route passing Grisedale Tarn before descending through a long valley to the village.

The final stage from Patterdale back to Ambleside climbs steadily to Scandale Pass, with a choice of routes to finish. The recommended route in good weather is to climb to Red Screes then follow a fantastic ridge all the way to the outskirts of Ambleside. An alternative, lower route directly descends from the pass to Ambleside.

PLANNING YOUR TOUR

The low-level Tour is suitable for most walkers with hillwalking experience, and it would suit active families with older children capable of walking for at least five hours each day. There are nine stages described, each taking between four and seven hours to complete. While strong walkers may be able to combine two shorter or easier stages, most people will want to allow a little more time, either to further explore some of the towns and villages or to split some of the longer stages over two days. This is easily achieved on every stage except Stage 5 between Buttermere and Keswick, and the final three stages of the Tour. The facilities tables in Appendix C and alternative schedules at the beginning of the book will help in planning to meet your needs, and there are also options to miss stages either with a shortcut walk, or by taking a bus if time is limited. These are clearly indicated at each stage.

WHEN TO GO

The Tour of the Lake District can be walked at any time of year, but it is better to avoid the winter months as weather conditions can make some sections very challenging and accommodation options may be limited. Remember also that during the winter

Stepping-stones can be impassable in winter, as seen here at St Catherine's Church near Eskdale (Stage 3)

months daylight hours are limited; if you're walking the Tour at this time of year you should adapt your daily plans accordingly.

The driest months are April, May, June and July, while the period from October to January tends to be wettest. Therefore the best months to walk the route are likely to be between April and September. Spring is a lovely time of year, and often relatively dry. The hills and valleys echo with the sound of bleating lambs, the grass and trees are vivid green, and the paths are clear and easy to follow. Summer can be crowded, with more pressure on accommodation, and some paths can be challenging to follow when hillsides are covered in bracken.

In general, you are likely to enjoy good weather for at least some of your Tour; however, bad weather can affect the region at any time of year, so be prepared with appropriate gear (see 'Equipment', below). Daily temperatures rarely climb above 20°C in summer – a comfortable temperature for walking. Winter walking can also be enjoyable provided you have the right clothing and experience, although

bear in mind that high-level routes are often thick with snow and sometimes ice.

Situated on the north-west coast of England, the Lake District often bears the brunt of wet and stormy weather brought on the prevailing south-westerly winds from the Atlantic Ocean. The weather can change very quickly in the mountains: a warm sunny morning can easily change within less than an hour, bringing a drop in temperature, strong winds and rain. High-level routes can be especially difficult in bad weather and poor visibility, so you should be confident in your navigation skills. Detailed three-day weather forecasts can be obtained from www.lakedistrictweatherline.co.uk and the Mountain Weather app and are normally pinned to noticeboards in walkers' accommodation.

Seathwaite in Borrowdale has the unenviable reputation for being the wettest inhabited place in the United Kingdom and receives around 3552mm (140in) of rain per year. Heavy rain will swell the myriad streams and rivers, sometimes making stream crossings challenging and obscuring stepping-stones under water.

HOW TO GET THERE

Train and bus services provide access to Windermere and Ambleside from the West Coast Main Line at Oxenholme Lake District station near Kendal. From the north there are bus services from Penrith railway station to Keswick and Patterdale, and onwards from Keswick to Grasmere, Ambleside and Windermere. International visitors will find Manchester Airport the most convenient, with regular train connections via Preston to Oxenholme, and on to Windermere. Carlisle Airport has regular flights from London, Belfast and Dublin, operated by Loganair.

If travelling to and from the Lake District by car, it is possible to buy a parking ticket for up to seven days (£31 in 2020) at the machine in the main Ambleside car park (for use in that car park only).

LOCAL TRANSPORT

For travel within the Lake District, the regular 555 bus service operates between Lancaster and Keswick, calling at Kendal, Windermere, Ambleside, Grasmere and other stops through to Keswick. This can be useful if time is short to leapfrog to later stages of the Tour. There is a seasonal bus service between Buttermere and Keswick via the Honister Pass, and also one linking Patterdale with Windermere, although at the time of writing this latter one is suspended due to COVID-19 restrictions. There is also a bus service between Coniston and Ambleside via Hawkshead, a service between the Old Dungeon Ghyll (Great Langdale) and Ambleside, and a regular service between Seatoller (Borrowdale) linking Rosthwaite and Keswick.

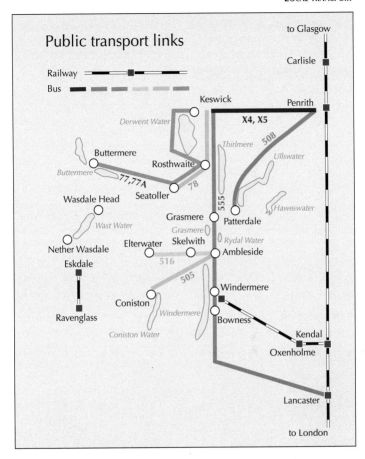

Public transport links

Railway

Bus

to Glasgow

Carlisle

Keswick

Penrith

X4, X5

Derwent Water

Thirlmere

508

Ullswater

Buttermere

Rosthwaite

Buttermere

77, 77A

78

Seatoller

Haweswater

Wasdale Head

Grasmere

Patterdale

555

Wast Water

Grasmere

Rydal Water

Nether Wasdale

Elterwater

Skelwith

Ambleside

Eskdale

516

505

Windermere

Coniston

Windermere

Ravenglass

Bowness

Kendal

Coniston Water

Oxenholme

Lancaster

to London

As the region is mountainous it is important to understand that connecting by taxi or bus from one valley to another can take a very long time, and in the case of a taxi can end up being quite costly, especially in the more remote western valleys.

Lake steamers operate on Windemere, Coniston Water, Derwent Water and Ullswater, making it possible to take short boat trips instead of walking, especially on Stage 5 on the approach to Keswick, Stage 6 on Derwent Water en route to

Rosthwaite, and between Ambleside and Windermere.

ACCOMMODATION

There is plentiful accommodation throughout the Lake District, although bear in mind that in the height of summer and at other peak times such as Bank Holiday weekends it may be difficult to find somewhere to stay. Booking well ahead is advisable. The main centres in the area are Windermere, Ambleside, Coniston, Keswick and Grasmere. Smaller villages include Elterwater, Seathwaite, Eskdale Green, Nether Wasdale, Buttermere, Rosthwaite and Patterdale, all of which have more limited accommodation choices.

Some hotels and inns require a minimum stay of two nights, but this can often be worked around by using public transport or a taxi to return to the route for the second day. Bed and breakfast accommodation is popular, and there are also options to stay in hostels, camping barns, camping pods and on campsites. Wild camping should only be done discreetly in the higher fells, and the site always vacated in early morning, leaving no trace. For legal guidance on wild camping, check the national park website (www.lakedistrict.gov.uk).

Hotel and B&B accommodation in the height of the summer season can be pricey, with a room and breakfast for two costing upwards of £80–100 per night, while campsites and camping barns are a much cheaper

Elterwater Youth Hostel (Stage 1), one of many popular accommodation options for families

There are plenty of excuses and opportunities to enjoy a snack on the way!

option, costing around £13 per person per night in peak season.

General B&B and hotel accommodation websites can be found in Appendix A, and a list of selected accommodation options is provided in Appendix B. The facilities table in Appendix C may also be useful in planning your overnight stays.

EQUIPMENT

What you take will depend on how you're planning your overnight stops. If you're camping you'll need a fairly large pack, to include a tent, sleeping bag and mat, and probably cooking equipment. If using the services of a luggage transfer company or on an organised walking holiday, then you'll just need a day pack in which you can carry essentials for the day. Staying in hostels will require a sleeping bag. For those without luggage transfer but with overnight accommodation booked ahead, the following kit list covers everything you'll need and should fit into a 30–40 litre rucksack. Remember to keep your kit to a safe but minimum level, as carrying extra weight will slow you down and make the whole trip less enjoyable.

- Rucksack: 30–40 litres for hostelling, 20–30 litres if using luggage transfer, or 50–60 litres for camping and backpacking.
- Rucksack cover, and ideally a liner of some sort. Consider using separate stuff sacks for groups of items – this allows you to keep organised and find things

quickly and easily. It also adds further protection against getting wet.

- Boots (or trail shoes if you genuinely prefer). The terrain is often rough and rocky, and there are boggy areas to cross, so comfortable waterproof boots that you know work well for your feet are the best option for this trip.
- Walking poles can provide additional stability and are highly recommended, as there are some occasionally awkward stream crossings.
- Waterproof jacket and trousers. Buy the best you can afford, as you may need to be using these all day, for several days.
- Hat, gloves and maybe a neck warmer for additional warmth
- Sun hat and sunscreen (in summer)
- Good-quality walking socks – two pairs ideally
- One or two fleeces or similar
- One long-sleeved and one short-sleeved base layer
- Two pairs of trousers, or one long and a pair of shorts or ¾ length
- Underwear
- Travel detergent for hand-washing clothes (most accommodation providers will provide drying facilities)
- Toiletries and any daily medication
- Spare shoes to change into in the evenings

- A good basic first aid kit – including blister plasters, tick remover, pain relief
- Whistle and torch
- Compass, maps and guidebook
- Mobile phone and charger (note that there are many places on the route where there is little or no signal. Remember to download anything critical such as mapping to use offline.)

You will also need to carry at least 1 litre of water each day – more in hot weather – as well as food and energy snacks.

In winter you'll need all of the above, but base layers will need to be winter-grade, and hats, gloves and additional outerwear will also be needed to provide sufficient warmth. Crampons or micro-spikes are advisable in winter, as is an ice axe for any high-level routes.

MAPS AND APPS

The mapping within this guide is extracted from Ordnance Survey Landranger 1:50,000, which is sufficient for generally following the route along with the route description. It is highly recommended that you also carry a map at a larger scale, to ensure accurate route finding and to allow for better navigation, especially in the higher fells and in poor weather. Almost the entire route is shown on the 1:25,000 Ordnance Survey AA Central Lake District Walker's Map (2); the only section not included on this map is part of the low-level route via Nether Wasdale on Stage 3. The Harvey/BMC Lake District map covers the entire area and route of the Tour at a scale of 1:40,000, so the scale is better than the Landranger 1:50,000, but not as clear as the OS AA Central Lake District map. For more comprehensive coverage of the Lake District, the OS 1:25,000 Explorer maps OL4, 5, 6 and 7 cover the north-western, north-eastern, south-western and south-eastern Lake District. Alternatively, the OS 1:50,000 Landranger maps required are sheets 96, 89 and 90. The disadvantage of these options is that you need to carry up to four maps, rather than just one!

There are a number of useful websites and apps which will help you get the best out of your visit and tour around the Lake District. These include mountain weather information, public transport apps, mapping and navigation apps, as well as information about accommodation, attractions and the national park in general. More details can be found in Appendices A and B.

NAVIGATION AND SAFETY

It's important that you are (or become) confident in the use of a map and compass for navigating in the mountains, and well-practised before you embark on the Tour. Even the lower-level main route regularly crosses passes well above 600m, and although the route generally follows well-defined paths, navigation in some remote and high places can be extremely difficult in heavy cloud or stormy weather. Cicerone's *Navigation* mini-guide can help you master the basics and refresh any lapsed skills.

As indicated in 'Equipment' above, a first aid kit is essential, as are decent-quality footwear (preferably boots) and waterproofs. Re-treat your gear to ensure the best performance.

Carry enough food for during the day, and always ensure you have a spare energy bar or snack at the bottom of your rucksack. Keeping energy levels topped up steadily throughout the day is generally much better than stopping just once to have a large lunch, especially if you have some climbing to do in the afternoon!

Although not essential, it is also recommended that you take a small emergency shelter. These can be very compact and lightweight – often just a bag made from 'space blanket' material.

Cicerone publishes a mountain safety leaflet for the Lake District in conjunction with the Lake District Search and Mountain Rescue Association. This clearly outlines everything you need to do in order to have a safe time in the mountains – such as checking the weather forecast before you set out; letting somebody know your intended route (this is often easy when trekking as you can tell your accommodation provider); taking a map, compass

COUNTRYSIDE CODE

Respect – Protect – Enjoy

Respect other people:
- consider the local community and other people enjoying the outdoors
- leave gates and property as you find them and follow paths unless wider access is available

Protect the natural environment:
- leave no trace of your visit and take your litter home
- keep dogs under effective control; bag and bin dog poo

Enjoy the outdoors:
- plan ahead and be prepared
- follow advice and local signs

Specific additional guidance can be found at www.gov.uk (search 'countryside code').

COVID-19

In addition, while the coronavirus pandemic continues, the following advice should also be noted:
- follow paths but give way to others where the path is narrow
- don't have BBQs or fires
- plan ahead, check what facilities are open, be prepared
- follow advice and local signs and obey social distancing measures.

and mobile phone; watching out for fatigue and dehydration; and walking at a pace that's suitable for all members of your group. There are also the emergency contact details. The leaflet can be downloaded from the Cicerone website: www.cicerone.co.uk/lake-district.

One of the best ways to guard against injury is to have spent time walking in your boots with the pack you'll be using, before embarking on your trip. Try to take several weekends walking back-to-back days over hilly countryside if possible, so that you know your boots will remain comfortable and your body is adapted and fit for the trek. Many callouts for the mountain rescue teams are from people who have injuries associated with a lack of sufficient training and hill fitness, as well as those who get lost. Good preparation will help to ensure that you do not need assistance – although if you do, details are indicated at the front of this guidebook.

Looking towards the Langdale Pikes from the lower slopes of Loughrigg (Stage 1)

USING THIS GUIDE

This guide describes a clockwise circular Tour of the Lake District, beginning and finishing in Ambleside, with an optional 'prologue' stage between Windermere railway station and Ambleside. For convenience, the route is divided into nine stages, with each stage ending at a location where there are a number of accommodation options. For fit and experienced walkers it is perfectly possible to walk the entire route in the nine days suggested, and some may find that a seven- or eight-day itinerary is both possible and more convenient. However, some of the stages are quite long, and it's worth remembering that this is a holiday and something to be enjoyed and relished. If you feel you would prefer to take the Tour at a slower pace there is everything to

be gained by not becoming overtired and giving yourself time to enjoy this beautiful region.

Clockwise or anti-clockwise? The Tour is described in a clockwise direction, providing the option to begin with a lower-level first stage that can easily be split into two before the first taste of the higher fells. Stage 2 as described can also be split at Dunnerdale, with camping options on the route and other accommodation further down the valley. If tackling the route in an anti-clockwise direction, there are no options to break the first three stages until Rosthwaite. Alternative itineraries for seven days and for 13 days are outlined, but these are just suggestions – it's your journey, and you will have different priorities and needs. A listing of the main accommodation, facilities and transport options for the entire Tour is also provided (see Appendix C) and may be useful in planning possible alternative stages.

Each stage begins with some information about the route. As well as the basics of distance, approximate walking time, ascent and descent, the high point for the day and any facilities on the route, there's also an introductory paragraph to give a flavour of the stage so you know roughly what to expect, and some suggestions for using transport options if time is short. A transport overview map is included in the guide, which should make these options easy to visualise.

Five of the nine stages have high-level, fell-top alternatives which can be mixed and matched according to the weather, your ambitions and energy levels. These can be highly rewarding and exhilarating days; however, there's little point in spending a high-level day in thick cloud – far better to save those summits for another day when you can enjoy the views. Remember that the fells will always be there, and it's a perfect excuse to return to the Lake District.

Places of note are highlighted in **bold**, corresponding to features shown on the map. Where possible, background information relating to some of the key landmarks and features visited on the Tour is provided.

Finally, there are appendices providing key contact information, useful websites and apps, accommodation providers, at-a-glance facilities on the route, and a reference of Lake District place names and their meanings.

Times and distances

Distances are quoted in kilometres, and heights are quoted in metres as shown on OS Explorer mapping, where one square is equal to 1km. The information box for each stage shows the total distance in both kilometres and miles. The walking times are a good indication of the time required to walk the stage, based on both actual recorded times and cross-checked with Naismith's rule (1hr per 4km plus 1hr for every 600m). Strong walkers will find they are quicker, while those with children, or those carrying full camping gear may need to allow a little more time. You should allow additional time for taking photographs, rest stops, lunch, consulting the map and guidebook and for admiring the views.

GPX tracks

GPX tracks for the routes in this guidebook are available to download free at www.cicerone.co.uk/1049/GPX. A GPS device is an excellent aid to navigation, but you should also carry a map and compass and know how to use them.

THE TOUR OF THE LAKE DISTRICT

Walkers pause to admire the view on the path from Scarth Gap to Buttermere (Stage 4/4A)

PROLOGUE

Windermere to Ambleside

Start	Windermere railway station
Finish	Ambleside
Distance	10.5km (6½ miles)
Total ascent	350m
Total descent	400m
Time	2hr 45min
High point	Robin Lane, 240m
Refreshments	Small shop on the route in Troutbeck; pubs off the route on the A592
Transport	555 bus to Ambleside; lake launch from Bowness-on-Windermere to Ambleside Waterhead
Accommodation	Ambleside has all services and plentiful accommodation

A surprising way to link these two big Lake District centres, and a good way to get a first taste of the lower fields and hills as you move towards the start proper of your Tour of the Lake District. The route is usually very quiet, with good views across to the Old Man of Coniston and the Langdale Pikes and down to England's largest lake. Halfway along, Townend is an interesting and well preserved old Lake District farmhouse and gardens, now owned by the National Trust.

From **Windermere station**, walk up to the main A591 road and cross over at the pelican crossing, then 10 metres to the left take the small road signed to Orrest Head that climbs steeply past houses. Stay on the tarmac through several switchbacks until you find a sign straight up to Orrest Head. Follow this and continue steeply to Windermere's great **viewpoint** (238m).

From the summit, head north down a steep rutted path. Take a stile through a wall and continue on the path across a meadow and descend into woods, coming out at a small road. Turn left and then right past cottages

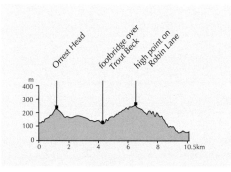

and enter open fields. The route here is fairly level. Cross three fields and come to the farm at **Far Orrest**. Pass through the farm and continue to meet a tarmac road. Almost straight across this, pass through another farm, then keep to a clear pathway across fields, meeting the **A592** Troutbeck road at Thickholme Bridge.

Cross the road and turn right along the pavement, which becomes a path alongside the road. Take the first left turn and descend steeply to **Trout Beck**. Cross a

View from Orrest Head towards Troutbeck and Red Screes

bridge then climb the track to a road and turn right past **Townend**. ▸ After five minutes, come to a small general store and a well-placed bench.

Turn sharp left on Robin Lane. This old turnpike is clearly signed and runs all the way to Ambleside. The climb is steep at first on a well-made track between field walls, but soon levels out. Wide views open up across Windermere and to the higher mountains. At a point where the main track appears to continue, take the descending path to the left signed for Ambleside. Cross the bridge at Low Skelghyll, pass the farm at **High Skelghyll**, and gradually descend into woods (**Skelghyll Wood**). ▸ If you want to visit Waterhead (for buses and steamers), drop down on a path to the left shortly after Jenkin Crag and a stream crossing, otherwise continue down through the woods, looking down on the garden centre, and soon reach a quiet road near the A591.

Turn right on the quiet lane that runs north parallel to the main road. It climbs slightly before dropping into **Ambleside**. The bus station is the first turn left. Otherwise continue along the road into the centre of the town for all shops and facilities.

Townend is a traditional Lake District stone and slate farmhouse dating back to the 17th century, displaying tools, furniture, a library and cottage garden.

Jenkin Crag, just off the trail, gives another fine viewpoint.

Approaching Far Orrest Farm

STAGE 1

Ambleside to Coniston

Start	Salutation Hotel, Ambleside
Finish	Bridge over Church Beck, Coniston
Distance	20km (12½ miles)
Total ascent	610m
Total descent	610m
Time	6hr
High point	Tarn Hows, 220m
Refreshments	Skelwith Bridge, Elterwater, Little Langdale
Transport	516 bus serves Ambleside, Skelwith Bridge, Elterwater (and on to Old Dungeon Ghyll Hotel); 505 bus runs between Ambleside and Coniston (via Hawkshead)
Accommodation	Hotel and nearby B&B at Skelwith Bridge; hotel, B&B and hostel at Elterwater; camping at Chapel Stile (off route); inn at Little Langdale; all types of accommodation at Coniston

Although this first stage of the Tour of the Lake District appears to avoid any major climbs, there are superb views from the high points reached and the accumulated ascent over the entire day is not insignificant. The route is full of interest, on low fells, waterside and woodland tracks and paths, passing delightful villages and some historic landmarks and buildings, including a farm once owned by Beatrix Potter. A brief detour at Hodge Close visits a huge and impressive quarry cavern with a water-filled bottom. The stage can easily be split into two shorter sections, with accommodation options at both Elterwater and Little Langdale, and camping at Chapel Stile (1km from Elterwater).

With your back to the Salutation Hotel in **Ambleside**, turn right, then cross the road and walk down Compston Road. At the next pedestrian crossing take the smaller road to the right, signed to Rothay Park and Loughrigg. Pass to the right of St Mary's Church and then go through

Map continues
on page 40

the park, with the playground to your left. At the far end
of the park, cross over the river on a beautiful old packhorse bridge to join a road.

Turn right, cross over a cattle grid, then immediately
turn left to begin to climb steeply, signed as a public bridleway. The metalled road becomes a track after a group
of houses, then continues to climb. Pass through a gate,
and after 25–30min the track becomes a path at Pine
Rigg. Pass through two gates and continue to climb to
a high point at 195m (2.3km, **40min**) with the slopes of
Loughrigg above, and good views to the south.

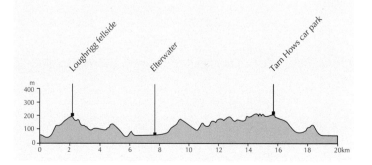

Windermere from the lower slopes of Loughrigg

Now begin a gentle descent following the main path, ignoring turns to the right and left. Some 10–15min from the high point the path divides. Ignore the smaller path rising to the right, but when the path divides again, take the right fork, keeping the stone wall to your left, and continue to descend.

Pass through a gate, now on the edge of larch woods, ignoring the first turn on the right. Pass through a gate at Tarn Foot Lodge and turn sharply right through another gate, signed High Close Estate, Loughrigg Tarn. The track passes above and to the right of the **tarn**, then take the path through a gate on the left, skirting the side of the field above the tarn. Go through a gate and then directly across the next field to meet a small road (5.2km, **1hr 20min**). Turn left.

The road rises, at the top of which turn right (signed Skelwith Bridge 1 mile). Pass in front of a pretty farmhouse (often with jam and other delights for sale) and take a path straight ahead to the right of the second house. Climb, with good views back down to the tarn and Loughrigg, then go through a gate and into the woods of the Neam Cragg estate, following footpath signs with yellow-topped posts among the holiday lodges and descending steeply. Go down a path to the road in front of the **Skelwith Bridge Hotel** (6.2km, **1hr 45min**).

Cross the road and walk round the hotel, then turn right towards Chesters café (vegetarian) and shop. Pass to the right of the shop and continue straight on between the river and the road. ▶ Follow the path (part of the Cumbria Way) as it meanders gently through the valley to arrive at **Elterwater** (8.8km, **2hr 30min**).

To the left is the Skelwith Force waterfall.

> **Elterwater** is a charming Lakeland village, its name derived from Elter Water, in the heart of Great Langdale. The Britannia Inn is the focus of the village and makes a good base for day walks in the area. The village also has B&B options, an independent hostel and a small seasonal shop/café.

Cross the river and fork left, turn right at the **Eltermere Hotel**, and climb steeply, first on a metalled road which shortly becomes a rough and steep stony track for just under 1km. At the high point, turn left through a gate signed Wilson Place ½ mile. Cross the field and then descend, passing through two fields and gates, to reach **Wilson Place Farm**. Pass to the left of the farm and walk down to meet a road (10.8km, **2hr 50min**). ▶

The Three Shires Inn (meals and accommodation) is 100 metres to the right.

Turn left, then almost immediately right at the first footpath sign by a house. Descend across the field and over a wooden footbridge, then climb towards a group of white cottages, passing through a gate and going up a path between two walls to reach **Stang End**. Turn left then immediately right on a track, which undulates and passes through two gates. After just over 500 metres from Stang End the path rises, just before a path junction. Turn right at the junction and go through a gate into woods (12km, **3hr 20min**). Walk through the woods to **Hodge Close**.

To view the quarry

For a short excursion, at Hodge Close continue ahead on the road for just under 100 metres to peer into the vast and awe-inspiring hole, filled with a deep pool – a spectacular reminder of the extensive slate quarrying in

the area. To rejoin the route, either retrace your steps to Hodge Close or walk round the deep hole to meet the track to High Oxen Fell.

High Oxen Fell Farm, one of several originally owned by Beatrix Potter

At Hodge Close fork left and immediately left again through a gate onto a track signed to High Oxen Fell. Pass through another gate and descend the rough track in a series of zigzags to reach High Oxen Fell Farm.

> **High Oxen Fell** has a 17th-century Grade II listed farmhouse, gifted to the National Trust by Beatrix Potter. The views from the farmhouse northwards are stunning.
>
> **Beatrix Potter** (1866–1943) developed a lifetime interest in natural history, animals and farming. Her first book, *The Tale of Peter Rabbit*, was self-published when she was in her 30s, and a further 22 children's books followed, the proceeds of which allowed her to buy Hill Top Farm in Near Sawrey in 1905. She became a prosperous farmer and over several decades purchased several more

farms in an effort to preserve the landscape, while breeding prize-winning Herdwick sheep. High Oxen Fell Farm, along with all her other farms, was bequeathed to the National Trust to continue to preserve this beautiful landscape for future generations.

From High Oxen Fell walk up the small road, bear right at a fork and then descend to meet the main Ambleside to Coniston road (13.6km, **3hr 45min**). Cross straight over the road (at Mole End cottage) and climb steeply up a metalled track, then fork right onto an undulating stony track, signed to Tarn Hows, and continue for 1km. Turn right through a gate in the wall, again signed to Tarn Hows, and go through woods to meet a path that circumnavigates the tarn a few minutes later. Turn right (or left) and head for the far southern end of the **tarn** to reach a small road and **car park** (16km, **4hr 40min**).

> **Tarn Hows** is a beauty spot owned by the National Trust. Surrounded by larch, pine and spruce trees planted in the 1860s, it was part of a broader area saved for the nation once again by Beatrix Potter. However, a recent severe outbreak of *Phytophthora Ramorum*, a fungus-like virus, has led to the felling of most of the larch trees surrounding the lake.

Ahead are views of the distant Langdale Pikes (Harrison Stickle and Pike of Stickle), with the bulk of Wetherlam ahead and the Old Man of Coniston to the left.

Turn right onto the road (the road is very narrow and one-way only – cars will approach from behind you). ◄ Walk downhill and after 400 metres turn right through a gate signed to Tarn Hows Cottages. Just before reaching the cottages, pass through a small gate ahead to enter **Tarn Hows Wood**, and descend steadily all the way to the valley, to emerge onto a riverside path.

Pass through a gate and, keeping to the right edge of the meadow, reach another gate. Continue straight on beside the river (**Yewdale Beck**) on a track. The track branches away from the river; as it begins to rise, take a path across fields to the right. Cross the first field and head into the second, keeping to the high ground on the left, then pass through two gates as you descend to the

village. Cross a stream by a house and turn left onto the road, then turn right at the next road junction and walk into the centre of **Coniston**, where the church is on the left and the bridge over Church Beck is seen directly ahead (20km, **6hr**).

Descending towards the village of Coniston, with Coniston lake beyond

> It is believed that **Coniston** (meaning 'The King's Manor') was once a Scandinavian (Norse) settlement, with Coniston Water originally known as Thurston Water. **Coniston Water** is the setting for Arthur Ransome's *Swallows and Amazons* books, and is also the lake on which Donald Campbell broke the water speed record on several occasions in the 1950s. Campbell died on the lake in 1967 while attempting to improve on his record time.
>
> In 1871 the famed art critic, painter and writer **John Ruskin** bought Brantwood, a stately house overlooking Coniston, and settled in the area. The Ruskin Museum in Coniston contains Ruskin memorabilia and items of local interest, as well as information about Donald Campbell.
>
> The village has hotels, B&B, pubs, cafés, shops, a youth hostel and nearby camping. Lake cruises are available on the restored steam-yacht Gondola.

STAGE 2
Coniston to Eskdale

Start	Bridge over Church Beck, Coniston
Finish	Doctor Bridge, Eskdale
Distance	18km (11 miles)
Total ascent	865m
Total descent	855m
Time	6hr–6hr 30min
High point	Summit of Walna Scar Road, 610m
Refreshments	Newfield Inn in Seathwaite
Transport	The Ravenglass and Eskdale Railway ('La'al Ratty'; privately owned) operates between spring and autumn; taxis can access the Duddon and Eskdale valleys
Accommodation	Camping and camping barn at Seathwaite; B&B at Ulpha (5km off route from Seathwaite); B&Bs, youth hostel and camping (including camping pods) in Eskdale. Note that some of the Eskdale options are into Stage 3; see note at end of route description.

On this stage you leave the relatively accessible village of Coniston and begin what will be three or four days in the more remote western fells, only reaching a town of any size when you arrive in Keswick at the end of Stage 5. The Walna Scar Road takes you high into the Coniston fells, with great views in all directions. Seathwaite makes a perfect stopping point for lunch, before tackling the second, easier climb of the day via Grassguards into Eskdale.

Note: It is possible to 'mix and match' the lower and higher routes on this stage, as both meet on the Walna Scar Road on the descent into the Duddon Valley. This would allow for an ascent of the Old Man of Coniston in the morning, or a visit to Hardknott Roman Fort in the afternoon.

From the centre of **Coniston**, facing the Black Bull Hotel, cross the bridge, bearing left to walk past a petrol station, then take the right turn up Station Road. This immediately swings right, then left to begin a steep climb – which will certainly wake you up first thing in the morning! After 700 metres the gradient begins to ease. Keep on the road, now in open country with pastures on each side and the Old Man of Coniston (803m) seen ahead. Pass through the gate at a small car park (1.2km, **35min**). For a short while the route – the **Walna Scar Road** – is generally easier, following a stone track with views all around as it crosses green pastures.

> The **Walna Scar Road** is an ancient route, possibly dating back to the Bronze Age. It was used as a packhorse route between Dunnerdale and Coniston to transport bales of wool during the Middle Ages, and to carry slate from the Coniston quarries.

At 280m elevation, about 8min (600 metres distance) from the car park, ignore the steep track to the right.

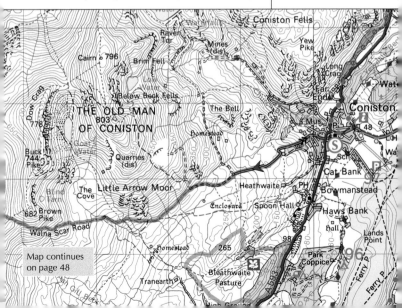

Map continues on page 48

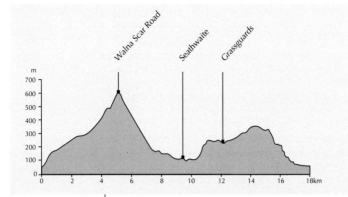

Continue ahead as the path now climbs again, passing through two narrow rocky sections. A path branches off to the right, heading for Goat's Water and the Old Man of Coniston; ignore this and continue ahead on the Walna Scar Road, crossing a packhorse bridge (Torver Bridge), with a steeper section seen ahead.

> The **views** from this spot are superb: to the right is a hanging valley – the Cove, flanked each side by Dow Crag and the Old Man of Coniston – while to the left are far-reaching views on a clear day down to Coniston Water and the coast of Morecambe Bay in the distance.

Climb steeply through zigzags, then across the flank of **Brown Pike** (682m) to reach the high point and a path junction at 610m (5.3km, **2hr**). Continue straight on. (The track to the right leads to the summit of Brown Pike and is the point where the high-level route from Dow Crag – Stage 2A– joins the Walna Scar Road.)

> The **views** from this point are extensive and dramatic. Ahead is the beautiful Duddon Valley, and to the right, in a north-north-westerly direction in the distance lies the huge mass of the Sca Fell range,

with Great Gable nestling behind. Ahead (almost due west) in the far distance on the coast is the site of the Sellafield nuclear power station.

Torver Bridge is crossed before the steeper climb to the high point on the Walna Scar Road

The descent is on a long, easy stone track to reach a ruined quarry building, then the track turns abruptly right to reach a gate, becoming grassy as it steadily descends, then stonier and rougher lower down. The roar of **Long House Gill** becomes increasingly loud, until finally a small road and bridge are reached (7.7km, **2hr 45min**). Here you have options.

To access Turner Hall campsite

If you are intending to camp at Turner Hall Farm, continue downhill from the bridge for about 200 metres then take the signed path to the left which crosses fields, passing to the right of a large house, then cross two further (larger) fields to reach **Turner Hall Farm**. From there a track leads to the road; turn left and walk to **Seathwaite**, 'the clearing by the lake', to rejoin the Tour.

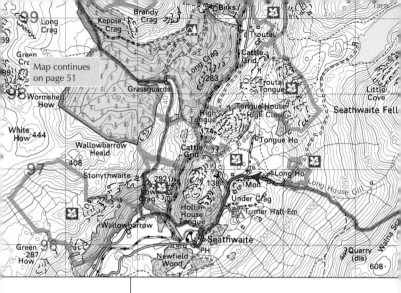

From the bridge it is also possible to reach Eskdale via Hardknott Pass and Roman Fort (see Stage 2A); however, for the lower route, walk straight down the road to meet the valley road and turn left. This leads straight to **Seathwaite** (9km, **3hr 15min**).

Direct route to Grassguards via Fickle Steps

For a more direct route to Grassguards via Fickle Steps (stepping-stones), turn right and walk north on the main valley road for 500 metres before dropping to the left to cross the River Duddon. Climb through woods, pass through a gate, then continue less steeply to reach a track just to the north of Grassguards. Note that this route is not safe during or after wet weather.

Take the path immediately opposite the Newfield Inn at Seathwaite, passing through three gates in close succession. Cross a field and then cross a stream on a narrow footbridge. Continue on the path roughly ahead (north) to reach a further footbridge and small sluice. The path now swings left across a field and into light woods, leading to an old packhorse bridge.

Cross the bridge, then take the path ahead and slightly up through the woods and onto a contouring path to **Wallowbarrow** (High Wallowbarrow Farm, seasonal bunkhouse accommodation), with views down into the valley. Turn right in front of the farmhouse, passing through a gate, and begin to climb, gently at first. After a second gate the climb becomes steeper, on a stony track with the roar of Rake Beck nearby and Wallowbarrow Crag looming above. ▶

Wallowbarrow Crag is a popular and accessible climbers' crag; you may well see climbers on it as you pass.

The path eventually takes a turn to the right by a wall, to begin a lovely traverse on a track over more open, rough moorland for just over 1km, passing through deer gates protecting an area of young trees, to reach a collection of two or three old but renovated cottages at **Grassguards** (12.4km, **4hr 10min**).

Do not cross Grassguards Gill but pass through a small gate, keeping the stream on your right as the path rises beside the gill. This small path is clear but often wet underfoot. Cross a track and a stream, then continue climbing steadily until the path crosses Grassguards Gill, and after a further 250 metres on a slightly boggier path, come to a path junction in woods. Continue straight

Looking back from High Wallowbarrow Farm towards Seathwaite

ahead, climbing gently to reach a high area at 350m elevation (14.3km, **5hr**).

The exact route of the next section of path is unclear in places, but generally descends in a north or north-west direction.

Pass through a gate and admire the view into Eskdale, with the Eskdale fells creating a backdrop and the Sca Fell range coming into view to the right. Gently descend the grassy path ahead, flanked by bracken in summer, then after 600 metres and a short boggy section find a stile on the left over the fence you've been walking next to, opposite a small crag (320m) (15.2km, **5hr 20min**). ◄

Cross over the stile and follow the path, which turns to descend alongside the fence line. Other stiles are passed. Hold close to the fence and descend a steep gully between rocky outcrops and the fence. At the bottom the path levels. A small post signs the path to the left; descend into a streambed with a single oak tree marking the crossing place.

Superb views towards the Sca Fell range on the descent into Eskdale

Cross the stream, then follow the path just above a wall, descending very slightly to reach a gate. Pass through the gate into a large field and continue on a grassy track to another gate. Go through a further field, still following the track, then through one final field to reach a gate leading to **Penny Hill Farm**. Walk through the farmyard

in front of the farmhouse (there is an optional permissive path (signed) to avoid the farmyard), then along the track to Doctor Bridge (18km, **6–6hr 30min**).

> **Doctor (sometimes 'Doctor's') Bridge** is a lovely single-arch bridge spanning the River Esk. Originally a narrow packhorse bridge, it was widened in 1734 by Dr Edward Tyson, a local surgeon, to take his pony and trap – hence its name.

Eskdale has various accommodation options spread throughout the valley. If you plan to take the high-level route over Scafell Pike the next day, then if possible, choose accommodation near Doctor Bridge. There are options at the Woolpack Inn and the youth hostel, B&B at Wha House Farm, and camping and camping pods nearby. If you are taking the main lower-level route, any accommodation between Doctor Bridge and Eskdale Green will be convenient. Walking time from Doctor Bridge to accommodation and camping options at Boot is around 40min, and walking time to Eskdale Green is around 1hr 40min. The only transport in the valley is the Ravenglass and Eskdale Steam Railway, which operates mainly between March and October – see https://ravenglass-railway.co.uk.

STAGE 2A

Coniston to Eskdale: high-level route

Start	Bridge over Church Beck, Coniston
Finish	Doctor Bridge, Eskdale
Distance	22km (13¾ miles)
Total ascent	1200m
Total descent	1190m
Time	8hr
High point	Old Man of Coniston, 803m
Refreshments	Newfield Inn in Seathwaite (off route)
Transport	The Ravenglass and Eskdale Railway ('La'al Ratty'; privately owned) operates between spring and autumn; taxis can access the Duddon and Eskdale valleys
Accommodation	Camping and camping barn at Seathwaite (off route); B&Bs, youth hostel and camping (including camping pods) in Eskdale. Note that some of the Eskdale options are into Stage 3; see note at end of route description.

This is a long stage taking in the Old Man of Coniston – the highest mountain in the southern Lakes – and providing the opportunity to visit the Roman fort at Hardknott. Paths over the Old Man are good and dry, while those passing the bulky Harter Fell are grassy and may be squelchy in places. Particular highlights are the quiet and little-visited Duddon Valley, and remote, beautiful Eskdale with views ahead to the Sca Fell range. This long day can be shortened by overnighting in the Duddon Valley at Seathwaite (5hr), or by using the main route either side of the shared descent on the Walna Scar Road (saving 30–40min).

Note: It is possible to 'mix and match' the lower and higher routes on this stage, as both meet on the Walna Scar Road on the descent into the Duddon Valley. This would allow for an ascent of the Old Man of Coniston in the morning, or to visit Hardknott Roman Fort in the afternoon.

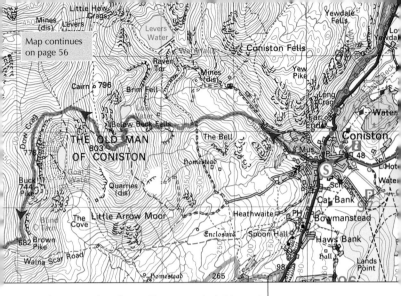

Map continues on page 56

From the centre of **Coniston** village, cross the bridge and take the small road signed to Coppermines Valley. Turn right by the Sun Inn and pass through an area of storage barns and workshops before starting to climb alongside **Church Beck**. After 30min reach Miners Bridge.

Alternative start

On the east side of the bridge in Coniston, take the first left turn along a small road which becomes a track and passes the house at Holywath before climbing gradually alongside **Church Beck**. At Miners Bridge, cross over and join the main route. (The track ahead leads to the youth hostel and cottages of Coppermines Valley.)

Continue along the path which now climbs above the upper beck, here called Levers Water Beck, with increasing views back down to the village and Coniston Water. Pass through two gates defining the Coppermines conservation area, with views over the buildings and impressively large spoil heaps generated by the extensive mining in the valley.

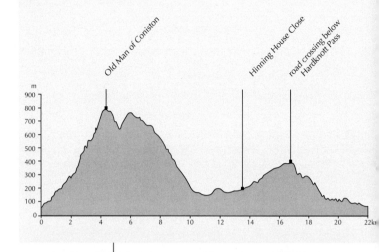

MINING IN THE CONISTON AREA

There are many metals and ores to be found in the Lake District, some of which are very rarely found elsewhere. Copper was the principal metal extracted not only from the mountains and hills west of Coniston, but also in Borrowdale, the Newlands Valley and the Caldbeck fells to the north. The main period of metal mining activity in the Lake District was between the late 16th and early 17th centuries, when copper, silver, lead and zinc, as well as many other precious metals, were extracted and smelted, particularly in the Keswick area, as well as Coniston. It was Queen Elizabeth I who had encouraged this, realising the economic possibilities of the industry, by establishing the Society of Mines Royal in 1568, by which she would be entitled to one-tenth of the native gold and silver, among other benefits.

Slate mining has also occurred for nearly 1000 years both in the Coniston fells and in the Skiddaw range in the north, providing strong and waterproof roofing materials in the immediate region as well as exports to all parts of Britain. The spoil heaps found in the Tilberthwaite valley between Little Langdale and Coniston are striking remnants of this industry. Slate mining continues today, as this natural stone continues to be one of the best materials for roofing.

The path climbs. Take care not to be diverted along the path that crosses between Walna Scar and Levers Water. Climb through an area of extensive abandoned mines, with cables used to haul the materials crossing the path. The going is stony, but the miners climbed this fully loaded daily and the gradients are tolerable.

At around 500m, approaching the tarn of **Low Water**, the path improves and becomes smoother. ▶ Continue to ascend, now more steeply, before coming out onto a broad ridge that climbs to the summit of the **Old Man of Coniston** (803m) (4.4km, **2hr 15min**).

Standing at a height of 803m (2632ft), the **Old Man of Coniston** is one of the highest fells in the Lake District, and one of the easier to climb, with several well-marked paths to the summit. It was once the highest point in the original County of Lancaster.

Take the broad path that descends gently north-west from the summit, bearing left after 250 metres, and descend to Goat's Hawse before climbing to the summit of **Dow Crag** (778m). ▶ Continue over the rise of **Buck**

Bird's-eye view of Low Water, with Levers Water and Wetherlam behind

The tarn is a beautiful heart-shaped gem buried in the crags, contrasting starkly with the upheavals below from the mining.

The vast rocks below were once the proving ground for Lakeland climbing.

55

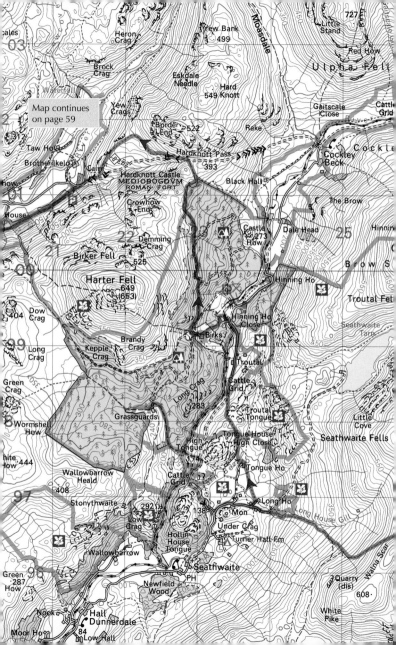

Map continues on page 59

Pike and then over **Brown Pike** to reach the junction with the **Walna Scar Road** at 610m (7.5km, **3hr 30min**).

Turn right (west) onto the Walna Scar Road, which makes a steady descent on the slopes to the west of the Coniston range. Initially the going is good but it becomes progressively stonier as the track descends to meet a metalled road at a bridge (10km, **4hr 15min**).

To reach Seathwaite and Grassguards

If staying in Seathwaite, continue ahead, drop to the valley road and turn left to reach either the campsite at **Turner Hall Farm** (1.5km from the bottom of the Walna Scar Road) or refreshments in **Seathwaite** 500 metres further on. From Seathwaite there is the option of following the main route (Stage 2) to Eskdale; if you choose to do this, a more direct way via Fickle Steps (stepping-stones) to Grassguards (not safe during or after wet weather) can be found by turning right along the main valley road and continuing for 500 metres before dropping to cross the **River Duddon**. After crossing the Fickle Steps, climb through woods, pass through a gate then continue (now less steeply) up to reach a track just to the north of **Grassguards**. Cross the stream and continue as described in Stage 2.

Continuing on Stage 2A, walk down the road and at the first houses take a lane to the right and follow this past **Long House**, crossing fields to Tongue House Farm. Here cross the steam (**Tarn Beck**) on a footbridge just south of the farm and climb past an isolated white cottage, then fork left shortly after to climb over a rise in a generally northerly direction before dropping to the road. Go north along the road for 1km and come to an old bridge at 175m, above a small gorge just to the south of a car park and picnic area at **Hinning House Close** (12.5km, **4hr 45min**).

Cross over the lovely old stone bridge spanning the gorge and pass through a gate. Continue on the path for 100 metres then turn left up through woods and emerge to cross open fields and reach the farm buildings at **Birks**.

Turn right in front of the farm buildings, pass through a gate and climb to reach a junction with a good track. Turn right, and after exactly 200 metres take a bridleway signed up to the left. (Although it is designated as a bridleway, the path is generally narrow and tends to be used mainly for walking.)

Initially the path is steep and stony, but then it eases and emerges from the trees near a viewpoint, after which it levels off for a further kilometre. On meeting a track cross straight over and continue, now on more open hillside, with good views across the Duddon Valley towards the Coniston fells, the steep slopes of Grey Friar opposite, and Wrynose Pass in the distance.

Cross a stream and continue to pass through a gate, then keep on the track, still heading mainly north until it turns right to reach a bigger gate in the fence 300 metres ahead. Go through this gate and continue straight ahead on the bridleway, swinging left once again in a northerly direction to a final rise before heading down to reach the road just to the west of the summit of **Hardknott Pass** (16.5km, **6hr 30min**).

Turn left and go downhill. The Roman fort is well worth a visit. Either descend the road to Jubilee Bridge, with an option to climb easily on a path from a small parking area to view the fort, or take a small path to the right at a hairpin bend after 200 metres on the road. This path can be hard to find if the bracken is high but makes a loop around the hillside before emerging first at the fort's parade ground and then at the impressive **fort** itself. In either case, allow an extra 15–30min to fully explore the fort.

Hardknott Fort was a garrison of the Roman Empire, with commanding views down the Eskdale valley towards the sea. At the beginning of the second century AD the Romans began construction of a major east–west road – known as the 10th Iter – to connect Kendal, Ambleside and Ravenglass, and the fort, known as Mediobogdum (the middle fort between Ravenglass and Ambleside) was built between AD120

and AD138 during the reign of Emperor Hadrian. It once housed not only the commander of the garrison, but barracks for several hundred men, granaries, a bathhouse, and a parade ground on the hill just above the fort towards the pass.

Part of the impressive remains of Hardknott Roman Fort

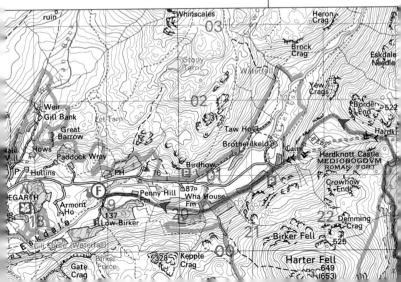

After visiting the fort, descend on a good path to the road, crossing a steep ladder stile near the bottom, and walk the few metres down to Jubilee Bridge (19.5km, **7hr**).

Cross the bridge – a tiny, charming packhorse bridge seen just to the left of the road by a small parking area – and after rising gently for a few metres take a small path branching to the right immediately after a gate. (If the bracken is high this turn can be easy to miss.) Continue alongside a wall under the shelter of trees, with occasional small climbs, then go through attractive woods before emerging at **Penny Hill Farm**. Take either the main path through the farm or a permissive path around it, before a final 400 metres down the farm's access lane brings you to Doctor Bridge (22km, **7hr 45min**).

Doctor (sometimes 'Doctor's') Bridge is a lovely single-arch bridge spanning the River Esk. Originally a narrow packhorse bridge, it was widened in 1734 by Dr Edward Tyson, a local surgeon, to take his pony and trap – hence its name.

If you plan to take the high-level route over Scafell Pike the next day, then if possible, choose accommodation near Doctor Bridge. There are options at the Woolpack Inn and the youth hostel, B&B at Wha House Farm, and camping and camping pods nearby. If you're taking the main lower-level route, then any accommodation between Doctor Bridge and Eskdale Green will be convenient. Walking time from Doctor Bridge to accommodation and camping options at Boot is around 40min, and walking time to Eskdale Green is around 1hr 40min. The only transport in the valley is the Ravenglass and Eskdale Steam Railway, which mainly operates between March and October – see https://ravenglass-railway.co.uk.

STAGE 3
Eskdale to Wasdale

Start	Doctor Bridge, Eskdale
Finish	Wasdale Head
Distance	18km (11 miles) direct route; 20km (12½ miles) via Nether Wasdale
Total ascent	470m
Total descent	460m
Time	5h–5hr 30min direct; 6hr–6hr 30min via Nether Wasdale
High point	Irton Fell, 280m
Refreshments	Eskdale Green, Nether Wasdale
Transport	Ravenglass–Eskdale Railway (between Dalegarth station and Fisherground Farm)
Accommodation	Hotel, inn, B&B, youth hostel and camping at Nether Wasdale; camping (including pods) at Brackenclose; inn, B&B and camping at Wasdale Head

The day begins with an attractive riverside walk through Eskdale, passing waterfalls and visiting St Catherine's Church, before heading through the beautiful Low Wood to Eskdale Green. From here the route climbs over Irton Fell with superb views into Wasdale, and then you can choose either the direct route through lovely countryside to Wasdale Head, or a detour via Nether Wasdale for refreshments and accommodation options.

Note: This is a relatively easy day with only a little climbing involved; however, it's still a long day, particularly if you take in a detour to Nether Wasdale. The route can be split at Nether Wasdale (3hr 20min) if preferred, allowing an option for a short stage to stay at Black Sail Youth Hostel – although this tiny remote hostel is often fully booked many weeks ahead. Nether Wasdale has two pubs, facing each other across the road. Both serve food and provide accommodation. Further accommodation is just up the hill, and there is also a campsite.

The main route involves walking up the side of Wast Water on the road, which might sound dull but is full of interest with good views throughout. The alternative is to use the 'Screes' path along the southern shore, but this will take at least an hour longer and maybe much more. It is a challenging alternative perhaps best avoided unless you have a set of unbreakable limbs!

From Doctor Bridge, pass through a gate onto the river path along the true right-hand bank. After 10–12min notice the lovely waterfall (**Birker Force**) above on the left. After a further 10min ignore a turn signed off to the right to Hows Wood. Continue ahead and through a gate (1.4km, **25min**).

Here you can choose either to visit the lovely St Catherine's church, or to take a more direct route via Gill Force. To view St Catherine's church, continue ahead with the river on your left. ◄

For accommodation and camping at Boot, go this way then take the track north from the church for 700 metres.

St Catherine's Church dates to the 12th century when the Priory of St Bees owned a chapel on this site. The font is decorated with ancient marigold designs, similar to those found on early Christian tombstones. The east window depicts St Catherine, the Good Shepherd and St Cecilia.

12th-century St Catherine's Church

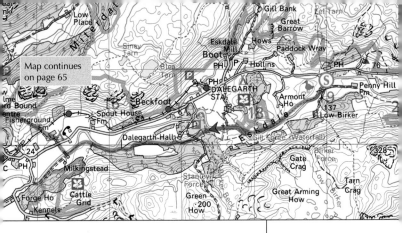

From the church, to continue on the main route towards Eskdale Green, cross on the stepping-stones (next to the church) to the other bank. However, during and after wet weather these stepping-stones across the River Esk will be impassable; if this is the case, after visiting the church, retrace your steps for 200 metres and cross on the wooden footbridge by **Gill Force**. Turn right and continue downstream.

Direct route avoiding St Catherine's church and stepping-stones

For a direct route via Gill Force, turn left onto the path by the river to view the **waterfall**, cross the footbridge, then turn right and keep following the river downstream until

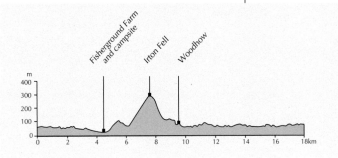

the stepping-stones opposite the church are reached and the paths reunite.

Continue ahead to reach a gate at a junction of tracks. Cross the footbridge and go straight through the gate ahead, moving away from the river across a field. Pass through another gate then go straight on across another field and into the lovely Low Wood. The path is clear to follow, all the way through the woods. After 5.1km (**1hr 30min**), reach a large metal barn on the left ('**Milkingstead**') and turn right to cross the suspension bridge. Cross the field, keeping to the left-hand side to meet the road (5.3km, **1hr 35min**).

Cross straight over the road and go up the track to **Fisherground Farm** (camping), passing just in front and then to the left of the farm buildings. Continue on the track, crossing the tiny **Eskdale Railway line**, and climb on the path on the other side, maintaining direction as you go. Pass through a gate in a wall and continue ahead, with woods to your left, to reach another gate in a wall. Turn left, and immediately afterwards meet a walled track at a right-angle bend. ◀

If you need provisions for the day, or camping and walking essentials, the Eskdale general store can be found by descending 200 metres to the left.

Turn right onto the track, passing **Low Holme**, and drop to a minor road (6.8km, **2hr**). Cross straight over, go through a gate and then cross the stream to begin a steady climb through the **Mitterdale Forest**. Numerous forest tracks will be crossed on the way up, but the bridleway is clear to follow, sometimes on ancient cobbles. There are occasional viewpoints where trees have been cleared.

Eventually the gradient eases and, crossing an open rough grassy area, it's apparent that you have reached the high point of **Irton Fell** at around 280m. Pass through a fence line, and shortly afterwards cross straight over a path junction with views down to Wast Water, and Nether Wasdale nestling in the valley a little to the left.

The descent on Irton Fell is steeper than the ascent, and quite wet and boggy in places, with a number of alternative 'paths' from which to choose to try to avoid the worst of the wet bits. A double gate through a wall is

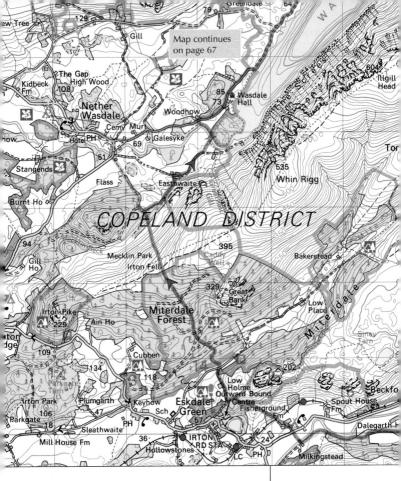

reached at the bottom of the fell, where you enter woods once again. Cross a stream, then after 200 metres reach a wall where there is a choice of routes (9.2km, **3hr**).

To visit Nether Wasdale

For refreshments or an overnight stay in Nether Wasdale, continue on the path ahead beside a wall, then after 100 metres fork right on a lovely path down next to the wall through light woods. Pass through a gate, cross a stream, then just to the right of **Flass Tarn**, pass through another gate and head directly towards a single white farmhouse. Reach a gate onto the road just to the left of the house.

Turn right, then branch left by the Sawmill Café and farm shop, then left again and walk into the village of **Nether Wasdale** (10.7km, **3hr 20min**), where there are further refreshment options and a range of accommodation.

To reach Wasdale Head, retrace your steps out of the village and fork left at the first junction, then continue straight along the road all the way up the valley beside **Wast Water**. There are fantastic views across the water to the Screes, and ahead to Yewbarrow, Kirk Fell and the slopes of the Sca Fell range. Wasdale Campsite is clearly signed at Brackenclose at the head of the valley on the right, and there are other accommodation options at **Wasdale Head** (20km, **5hr 30min**).

A good grassy track leads to Easthwaite Farm, with Yewbarrow and Great Gable seen clearly at the head of Wasdale

To avoid Nether Wasdale and continue directly to Wasdale Head, turn right where the path reaches the wall in the woods near the bottom of Irton Fell, pass through a gate and continue along a lovely grassy track with the wall on your left. Descend easily to **Easthwaite Farm** with wonderful views towards Wasdale Head and Yewbarrow ahead. Take the path down to the left of the farm buildings, then turn right through the farmyard area and continue on the track across fields for 500 metres, passing

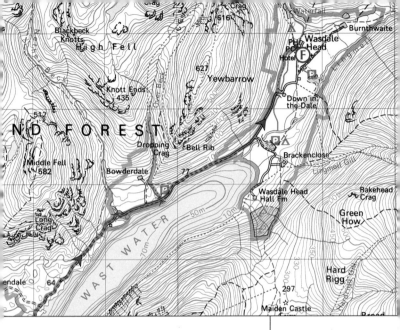

through three gates. Immediately after the third gate, take the path left down the field with a hedge on the left, to meet the **River Irt**.

Turn left and walk beside the river, then cross on the bridge and walk up the track with the river now on your left. Go straight up the field to reach the road opposite a complex of houses at **Woodhow**. Turn right and walk all the way beside **Wast Water** to arrive at **Wasdale Head** (18km, **5hr**).

Wast Water is England's deepest lake, with a maximum depth of 79m (258ft). The situation is dramatic, and reminiscent of Scottish scenery, the grandeur of the mountains surrounding the lake matched by the remoteness of the area. On a sunny summer day you will not feel lonely, however, as numerous cars and day-trippers will be negotiating the single-track road up the side of the lake to Wasdale Head.

STAGE 3A
Eskdale to Wasdale: high-level route

Start	Doctor Bridge, Eskdale
Finish	Wasdale Head
Distance	17km (10½ miles)
Total ascent	980m
Total descent	970m
Time	6hr 30min
High point	Scafell Pike, 977m
Accommodation	Camping (including pods) at Brackenclose; inn, B&B and camping at Wasdale Head

This stage to Wasdale Head explores Upper Eskdale, approaching Lakeland's highest mountain through its remotest valley. For some hours you draw nearer to Scafell Pike, Sca Fell, Esk Pike, Bow Fell, Crinkle Crags and other mountains from their wild side where relatively few walkers venture.

Scafell Pike is England's highest mountain, and this high-level route provides a perfect opportunity to bag it – as well as its sister peak, Sca Fell, if you have the time and energy – before descending to Wasdale Head. (The optional climb to Sca Fell involves an additional 250m of ascent and descent over difficult ground.)

The route does have some challenges – Great Moss is exactly as it is named and needs some care as you pass the edges of the large, flat, wet bog. The crossing of the upper Esk beck is usually unproblematic, and the initial part of the climb alongside Cam Spout waterfall is rocky and steep but should not cause difficulties and is soon passed. Take extra care with route finding after Mickledore on the way to the summit of Scafell Pike. Overall, this challenging route is best done in good weather.

Facing east, cross Doctor Bridge and bear left on the farm track to **Penny Hill Farm**. (An alternative path heads right, avoiding the farm.) Take the track bearing right after the farm buildings and follow this into fields, and at the first turn keep to the lower path. After 15min enter woods.

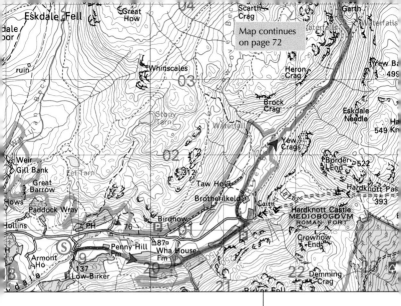

Map continues on page 72

The path climbs and drops, crosses a stream and passes paths to left and right. Continue straight ahead after the woods and through the bracken-covered hillside, then

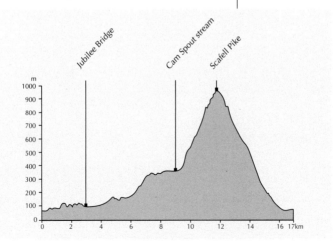

69

alongside a wall under trees, before emerging by a gate. Drop down a few steps and cross Jubilee Bridge (2.5km, **45min**).

Turn left down the road, cross the cattle grid, and at the bottom of the hill near an old red phone box turn right. ◀ Take the farm track to **Brotherilkeld Farm**. Keep left on the path and pass by the bridge to **Taw House**. Continue up the valley, either alongside the river or, drier and better, on the track then path that skirts the bottom of the hillside, with views ahead to the 'back' of Bow Fell and Crinkle Crags. After the paths merge, continue along the good path to Lingcove Bridge (185m) (5.8km, **1hr 45min**).

Numerous rights of way are shown on the map hereabouts, but actual paths are rarer. Cross the bridge and keep on the path to the left, with the **Esk** to your left. Several waterfalls in the gorge below can be heard but need a digression to see. Climb under Throstlehow Crag and **Scar Lathing** and emerge on to **Great Moss**. ◀ The path keeps to the riverside but is intermittent on the ground so you may need to make your own route. Pass under **Cam Spout Crag** (which is on the other side of the

An alternative start in the early morning would be to walk along the quiet road from the Woolpack Inn to the turn into the Brotherilkeld valley, saving 20min.

From here there are good views ahead to Esk Hause and Esk Pike.

Looking across Great Moss towards Esk Hause, with Esk Pike to the right and Scafell Pike to the left (photo: Joe Williams)

river) and find a suitable place to cross the Esk, and then immediately cross to the north side of Cam Spout Stream at 369m (**3hr**).

Follow the path alongside the north side of this beck. Initially grassy, it soon becomes rocky and steeper. There are a variety of routes up, keeping close to the stream. After a stiff 100m climb the path relents and becomes grassy again, climbing steadily to the **Mickledore** col between Scafell Pike and Sca Fell.

Mickledore, with Broad Stand and the dramatic crags of Sca Fell

> Sca Fell, Scafell Pike and the surrounding range provide one of the best **climbing and mountaineering** areas in England, with superb rock conditions and challenging classic routes, including Woodhead's Climb, Hopkinson's Gulley, Knife-Edge Arête, Moss Ghyll Grooves and Slingsby's Chimney. In recent times, local climber Dave Birkett has put up two routes graded E9 (an exceptionally difficult UK grade of climb) on Sca Fell's East Buttress.

To climb Sca Fell

Sca Fell is only 13m lower than the Pike. If you want to bag this impressive but relatively little-frequented peak,

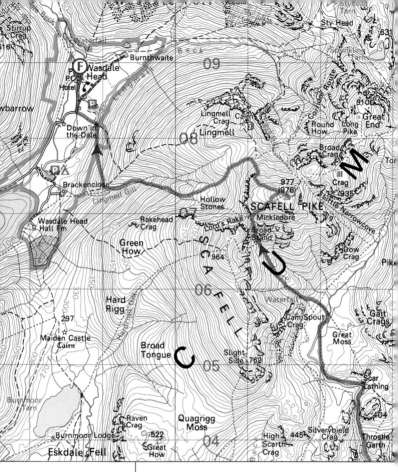

You are unlikely to be alone: claiming the summit is a popular activity, especially on weekends and sunny summer days.

take a small path to the left (west) below the final pull to Mickledore and head via Foxes Tarn (marked on the 1:25,000 map) to the **summit**. Return the same way (other routes are not recommended for walkers).

From Mickledore take the prominent path right that climbs steadily over the rocks to reach the summit of **Scafell Pike** (977m) (11.8km, **4hr 30min**). The summit is a large shelter built into a platform. ◄

The described descent takes the main ascent route from Wasdale. This is a large path, currently cut up and stony for most of the way, although repairs are in progress. It seems to take a long time to get down (this description assumes 2hr). Take the main path, heading north-west at 285 degrees. Initially and in poor weather it can be unclear, but it soon becomes a substantial and clear, almost unmissable track. Follow this down past Lingmell Col and the area known as **Hollow Stones**. Cross **Lingmell Gill** and continue down. At a gate the path splits: the left turn descends directly to the **Brackenclose** campsite and the right turn drops to **Wasdale Head** with camping and accommodation (17km, **6hr 30min**).

> **Wast Water** is England's deepest lake, with a maximum depth of 79m (258ft). The situation is dramatic, and reminiscent of Scottish scenery, the grandeur of the mountains surrounding the lake matched by the remoteness of the area. On a sunny summer day you will not feel lonely, however, as numerous cars and day-trippers will be negotiating the single-track road up the side of the lake to Wasdale Head.

Other descent options

Experienced walkers who know Scafell Pike and wish to avoid the 'tourist track' descent have a couple of options:

- Return to Mickledore and descend the west side of the col towards Wasdale. This is initially very steep so care is needed. It joins the main descent in Hollow Stones.
- From the Lingmell col between Scafell and Lingmell, find a path heading east. **Do not take the Piers Gill path** (which runs north-north-west) but continue north-east on the higher route known as the Corridor Route to Sty Head and descend the main path from there to Wasdale Head. This adds 45min to the descent.

STAGE 4
Wasdale to Buttermere

Start	Wasdale Head
Finish	Buttermere
Distance	12km (7½ miles)
Total ascent	780m
Total descent	750m
Time	4hr 30min–5hr
High point	Black Sail Pass, 558m
Accommodation	Youth hostel at Black Sail; hotels, B&B, youth hostel and camping at Buttermere

Although fairly short, this is a truly memorable day, as you climb out of the dramatic scenery of the Wasdale valley and drop into remote Ennerdale before climbing over a further pass to reach the Buttermere valley. The path from Wasdale Head keeps close to the Mosedale Beck as height is gained, first slowly and gently, then more steeply beside Gatherstone Beck (the crossing of which can be slightly tricky during and after wet weather) as it leads to Black Sail Pass. The descent path into Ennerdale is mostly clear to follow, with occasional piles of stones indicating the route. In wet weather the ground becomes quite boggy, and a short rocky step needs to be negotiated, which is particularly slippery when wet. The route passes the tiny hostel at Black Sail, nestling high in the Ennerdale valley, and after a short climb over Scarth Gap between Hay Stacks and High Crag the descent yields superb views into the beautiful Buttermere valley.

Note: This is a very remote corner of the Lake District. If for any reason you are not able to undertake this stage, alternative options are to hire a taxi from Wasdale Head to take you to Buttermere, or take the lower and easier Sty Head Pass route east from Wasdale Head to Seathwaite in the Borrowdale Valley, with options by bus from Seatoller (around 3hr). The nearest public road access to the Black Sail youth hostel is 4km away.

Map continues on page 78

BUTTERMERE

dale Edge

16

Hassness

Burtness Wood

Gatesgarth

Peggy's Bridge

104

115

Cross

Gatesgarthdale Beck

155

Chapel Crags

Bleaberry Tarn

807

806 High Stile

Grey Crags

Burtness Comb

Sheepbone Buttress

744

High Crag

BUTTERMERE FELL

Warnscale Bottom

648

Fleetwith Pike

Hon
Cra

Waterfall

Fle

Seat 561

Hay Stacks

697

Blackbeck Tarn

13

Pillar Rock

Robinson's Cairn

Pillar

892

Wind Gap

828

841

627

Looking Stead

Black Sail Pass

Black Sail Hut

Boat How

Kirkfell Crags

Moses Trod

Gillerc
H

Mosedale

19

802

Kirk Fell

20

899

Great Ga

821

Red Pike

Black Beck

17

18

Mosedale Beck

Wasdale Fell

Napes Needle

650

600

Low Tarn

Scoat Tarn

Gosforth Crag

Dore Head

Stirrup Crag

616

Waterfall

Beck

09

h Fell

627

Yewbarrow

Knott Ends
435

Gill

PH
Ho

S

Wasdale Head

Burnthwaite

P

Down in
the Dale

Lingmell Crag

Lingmell

08

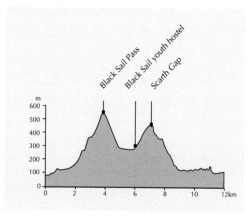

The valley is surrounded by the iconic peaks of Dore Head and Red Pike to the west, Kirk Fell to the east, and Pillar straight ahead.

From **Wasdale Head**, pass behind the hotel on the path keeping to the right of the Mosedale Beck, then fork left and climb gradually into the huge bowl of Mosedale. ◄ The clear path continues gently, then forks right through a gate to begin to rise more steeply, joining Gatherstone Beck as it tumbles energetically into the valley.

After just over 2km from Wasdale Head, the path runs close by the beck: look for the point where it crosses to the other bank by a large pile of stones. (An indistinct path continues for a while but there is nowhere good to cross the stream above, so retrace your steps if you have missed the correct crossing point.) During and after heavy rain this crossing can be difficult, but you are never in any danger – except perhaps of getting a bootful of water!

From the stream crossing the path climbs steeply to gain a small ridge, then continues with the stream now on the right. The gradient eases briefly before increasing again as **Black Sail Pass** is reached at 545m (4km, **1hr 45min**).

The descent into Ennerdale continues directly ahead, mostly quite steeply over rocks, grassy tussocks and numerous eroded paths. The path swings right to join Sail

Beck as it descends, crossing a slightly awkward small rock step before the gradient eases as the bottom of the valley draws near. Cross the stream (**River Liza**) on a footbridge then turn left and ascend to the **Black Sail youth hostel** (6km, **2hr 45min**).

From the tiny hostel, walk north-west down the track for about 5min, then on reaching a large gate across the track take the stone-pitched path to the right, climbing next to a fence initially, and then directly (but now less steeply) to **Scarth Gap**. Where a path crosses, linking High Crag and Seat with Hay Stacks (this is where the high-level route, Stage 4A, joins), continue ahead following the clear path marked with occasional piles of stone. Descend steeply for a while, then the gradient eases as you begin to enter the Buttermere valley.

Continue steadily down, eventually bearing left to join the level lakeside path that runs along the southern shore of **Buttermere**. Choose either the higher or lower route where the path splits, as these rejoin at the far end of Buttermere (the higher left fork is the main path). Cross two wooden footbridges at the head of the lake, then follow the level path between fields to enter the village of **Buttermere** (12km, **4hr 45min**).

Recently shorn Herdwicks graze on the slopes below Hay Stacks, on the descent path from Scarth Gap

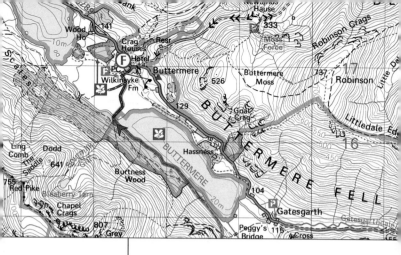

Buttermere, meaning 'the lake with rich butter pastures', occupies a level site of fertile land which splits a once single lake into two: Buttermere and Crummock Water. Surrounded by a superb range of mountains, the village is little more than a small collection of houses and farms, but with hotel and hostel accommodation and a campsite, making it an ideal base for a walking holiday.

Enjoying a well-earned rest at the Black Sail youth hostel

STAGE 4A

Wasdale to Buttermere: high-level route

Start	Wasdale Head
Finish	Buttermere
Distance	16.5km (10 miles)
Total ascent	1150m
Total descent	1110m
Time	6hr 30min
High point	Great Gable, 899m
Accommodation	Youth hostel at Black Sail; hotels, B&B, youth hostel and camping at Buttermere

This outstanding high-level crossing between two beautiful valleys takes in two iconic Lakeland mountains – Great Gable and Hay Stacks, the latter most famous for being Alfred Wainwright's favourite. It's a full day's walk, with lots of interest and fine views throughout. The climb to Sty Head takes a lesser-used path that rises easily, and the ascent of Great Gable is on a finely constructed trail. After a steep descent and then a climb to Green Gable, the route skirts Brandreth and heads cross-country to the shaggy rocks of Hay Stacks before dropping into the Buttermere valley. In poor visibility, the navigation between Green Gable and Hay Stacks will need care, and the descent from Hay Stacks is steep over rocky ledges, so another descent route is also described.

Facing east with your back to the inn at **Wasdale Head**, turn left and immediately right on a path crossing fields to the tiny St Olaf's Church. (If approaching from Brackenclose, take the footpath to Wasdale Head and branch right at the end of the car park along a track to reach the church.)

St Olaf's Church is England's smallest parish church, dedicated to the ancient king and patron saint of Norway. The current building dates from

Map continues on page 84

BUTTERMERE

BUTTERMERE FELL

Hassness

Burtness Wood

Goat Crag

129

727

Littledale Edge

Neal Tongue

Dalehea Crags

753

Dale Head

16

Gatesgarth

104

Peggy's Bridge

115

Cross

Gatesgarthdale Beck

155

Yew Crag

Grey Crags

Burtness Comb

Sheepbone Buttress

744

High Crag

Warnscale Bottom

648

Fleetwith Pike

Honister Crag

218

Mine Adventures

356

Se

Seat

561

Scarth Gap Pass

697

Hay Stacks

Waterfall

Fleetwith

13

Black Sail Hut

Blackbeck Tarn

Grey Knotts

697

Robinson's Cairn

Looking Stead

627

Boat How

715

Brandreth

Gillercomb

Base Bro

646

Black Sail Pass

19

Kirkfell Crags

Moses Trod

Gillercomb Head

18

Black Beck

802

Kirk Fell

20

801

Windy Gap

899

Aaron Slacks

Green Gable

21

sdale

Wasdale Fell

Napes Needle

Great Gable

Sty Head

759

Sprinkling

Stirrup Crag

616

Waterfall

Burnthwaite

Mosedale Beck

09

Corridor Route

Corridor Route

ore ead

Yewbarrow

627

S

Wasdale Head

Hotel

PC

Down in the Dale

Lingmell Beck

Lingmell Crag

Cam

Lingmell

Round How

Long Pike

G E

11

Great Gable area map

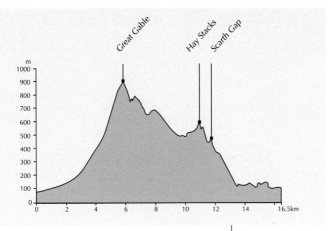

1550, although there is a suggestion that there has been a church on the same site since AD950, when Norse farmers settled in the valley from Ireland and the Isle of Man, bringing Christianity with them. On a stained-glass window in the church there is an etching of Napes Needle, along with an inscription that serves as a memorial to members of the Fell & Rock Climbing Club who died during World War 1: 'I will lift up mine eyes unto the hills from whence cometh my strength' (Psalm 121).

Continue along the track to the farm at **Burnthwaite**. The track is directed to the left of the buildings and continues across fields. Cross a beck on a good bridge and after about 300 metres find a path bearing right to continue alongside **Lingmell Beck**. The route straight ahead leads to Sty Head on the substantial and dull main path; instead, the lower route (an old pony route to Sty Head) is recommended. Much of the path is grassy, although it is stony in the flat lower section.

Stay on the beck-side path until you reach a confluence of streams, and cross on stones (marked 'Ford' on the 1:25,000 map). If the crossing is awkward there may

Looking south-west from Sty Head towards Piers Gill and Lingmell

be easier places just above the 'ford'. The path then rises steadily on a grassy trod, recrosses Spouthead Gill and emerges at **Sty Head** close to the stretcher box (475m) (4.3km, **1hr 30min**), with Great Gable looming above.

In June 1886, WP Haskett Smith soloed the first ascent of the rock pinnacle now known as Napes Needle on the southern flank of Great Gable. There are a number of other **classic climbing routes** found on both the southern and northern sides of Gable.

Take the Gable path, which starts 20 metres west of the stretcher box. It has been improved greatly and climbs craftily engineered steps most of the way up Great Gable, only becoming rough as you emerge onto the summit hump. Continue to the summit rocks of **Great Gable** (899m) (5.8km, **2hr 30min**).

Located on the summit of Great Gable, a **memorial** commemorates the lives of 20 members of the Fell & Rock Climbing Club who fought and died in World War 1. This replacement plaque was erected in 2013; the original is now housed in the Armitt Museum in Ambleside. Also commemorated is the acquisition of the surrounding fells by members, who gave the land to the National Trust.

To leave the summit, take a smaller path than the ascent route, heading north-east then turning east. This crosses the stony ground before starting to descend above crags. The route ahead becomes clearer, with the Green Gable path seen etched in red. Before reaching the well-named Windy Gap, drop steeply though a narrow gully, taking care if this is icy or wet. From **Windy Gap**, climb the short 50m to the summit of **Green Gable** (801m) (6.6km, **3hr**).

Although Great Gable is a fine viewpoint, it is possible that its lower cousin is even better, with **360-degree views** including Gable itself and the full panoply of northern, eastern and southern peaks as well as the Sca Fells.

From Green Gable take the path north-east, which then swings in a northerly direction. Hay Stacks is clearly seen but looks a long way below; on a day of poor visibility a compass bearing might help as, for an essentially straight route, it is awkward to follow on the ground. After 400 metres keep on paths to the left along a line of boundary posts ('BP' on the 1:25,000 map). (Heading east would take you to Seathwaite in Borrowdale, which is very nice but not where you need to go today.) A series of parallel paths head north; it is not crucial to get exactly the right thread, but after passing a group of small tarns the path starts to climb Brandreth, and a cairn marks the start of a small path to the left. Take this.

Skirt beneath **Brandreth** and come to a line of fence posts. ▶ Turn left down the fence line – the east (far) side is probably best – and pass a number of stiles over the fence. Descend on fairly wet ground, passing a gate through the fence where a path rises from Loft Beck – a route from the Black Sail hostel in Ennerdale. Just after the fence turns 90 degrees to the left, continue north-north-west on the path ahead. This passes close to the outcrop of Great Round How before meeting a larger path at 490m (9.5km, **4hr**).

Ahead are the slate mines of Honister, their workings clearly visible.

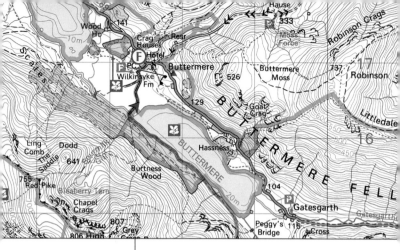

Turn left and follow the path towards Hay Stacks. The path rises and falls, passing **Blackbeck Tarn** before coming to Innominate Tarn (10.5km, **4hr 40min**), just below the summit. Keep climbing to reach the summit of **Hay Stacks** (597m), marked by what remains of a pole.

Alfred Wainwright was a keen fellwalker who explored the Lake District extensively, writing a

Walkers on the summit of Hay Stacks, with Grasmoor, Crag Hill and Sail seen in the distance behind

collection of seven guidebooks to the fells. He also devised and wrote a guidebook for a coast-to-coast walk across northern England. Born in 1907, he lived and worked in Kendal, and his favourite fell is said to have been Hay Stacks. There is a memorial to him in nearby Buttermere.

There are two descent possibilities. For the direct option, continue 50 metres past the summit, lining up the summit post and the east edge of a tiny tarn – this takes you to the top of the descent route, marked by a cairn. Drop down a ramp and ledges. After the initial drop the way is clear, but if you're heavily laden or the path is wet or icy and balance is awkward, you may prefer to take the left-hand route just beyond the tarn, which drops on an eroded but easier path. Both options merge at **Scarth Gap** (445m) (12km, **5hr 10min**), at this point also joining the Stage 4 lower-level route.

Turn right and take the path heading north into the Buttermere valley. Higher up this path is quite rough, but it then becomes easier on an improved trail. Continue down, looking over the flat fields at the head of Buttermere. Just before the bottom, take a path that continues straight ahead while the larger trail drops to the right along the side of a small isolated wood directly to Peggy's Bridge.

Emerge onto the lakeside path. This well-made trail leads along the shore of **Buttermere** with views across the lake to the crags low down on Robinson. At the end of the lake, turn right across a bridge and follow the path into the village of **Buttermere** (16.5km, **6hr 30min**).

Buttermere, meaning 'the lake with rich butter pastures', occupies a level site of fertile land which splits a once single lake into two: Buttermere and Crummock Water. Surrounded by a superb range of mountains, the village is little more than a small collection of houses and farms, but with hotel and hostel accommodation and a campsite, making it an ideal base for a walking holiday.

STAGE 5

Buttermere to Keswick

Start	Bridge Hotel, Buttermere
Finish	Moot Hall, Keswick
Distance	16km (10 miles)
Total ascent	490m
Total descent	515m
Time	5hr
High point	Saddle between Sail and Ard Crags, 470m
Refreshments	Swinside (1km off route), Nichol End, Portinscale
Transport	Summer bus service 77/77A from Buttermere to Keswick via Honister and Rosthwaite; Keswick Launch (Derwent Water) from Hawes End and Nichol End to Keswick
Accommodation	B&B (inn) at Swinside (1km off route); bunkhouse at Skelgill; hotel and B&Bs at Portinscale; all facilities at Keswick

This stage is characterised by a long, steady climb to the high point at around 470m – the watershed between the Sail Beck and Rigg Beck valleys. Views are good throughout, and there is little difficulty either in steepness or terrain. On reaching and crossing the Newlands Valley, the Tour crosses farmland below Cat Bells before joining the route of the Cumbria Way and the Derwent Water Walk through woods and meadows, touching the shore of Derwent Water before arriving in Keswick. There are very few facilities and no accommodation along the route until Derwent Water is reached. An option to save tired legs would be to take the Keswick Launch from Hawes End or Nichol End Marine to Keswick, saving around 2–4km (except in winter – see Appendix A for contact details).

With your back to the Bridge Hotel in **Buttermere**, turn left and walk up the road to reach Crag House Farm and a group of houses. Immediately past the farm, turn right and take the right-hand path running behind a line of cottages. Pass through a gate, following the path that keeps

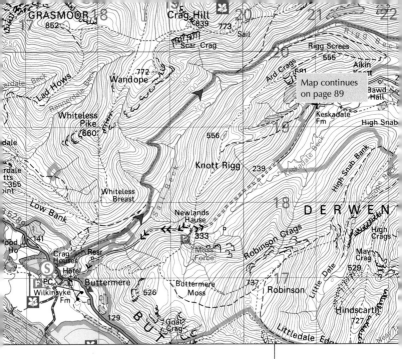

Map continues
on page 89

Setting out from Buttermere

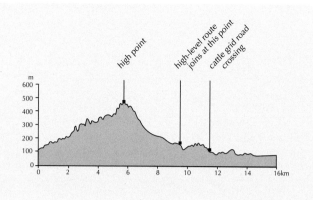

high point

high-level route joins at this point

cattle grid road crossing

close to a fence and later a wall. At a path junction ignore a smaller path rising to the left and continue on the main path, rising very slowly with emerging views.

After 30–35min look for a pile of stones at a path junction opposite a confluence of streams (Mill Beck and Swinside Gill) seen to the right. Take the path rising to the left. This soon curves to the left, steepening for a while,

Causey Pike seen directly ahead from the high point

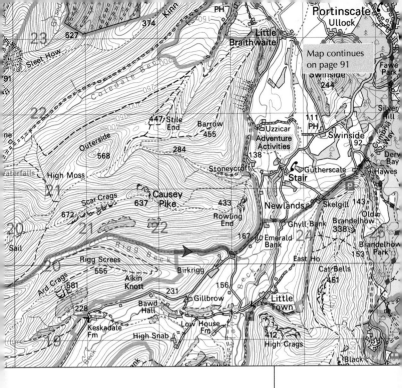

to enter a side valley. Cross the stream and climb out of the side valley onto a hillside of grass and bracken. Enter another side valley (called Third Gill) and again cross the stream and climb out of this side valley. The path contours around the hillside to a further gill which you cross, after which the path steepens for the final climb to the nameless pass at about 470m between Sail and Ard Crags, with Causey Pike seen ahead (6km, **2hr**).

The initial descending path passes through boggy ground, then across the top of a series of sections of scree. The path now descends more steadily with **Rigg Beck** just below and to the right, eventually reaching the Newlands road at a small disused quarry, with a stone bridge and impressive house hidden in the trees opposite (9km, **3hr**). Turn left and walk down the road for 10min

The high-level route joins at this point.

(800 metres), then turn right through a gate onto a path signed to Ghyll Bank. ◀

Descend to cross **Newlands Beck** on a bridge, then climb through a boggy field to **Ghyll Bank**. Turn left on the road then almost immediately right over a stile in a wall to follow the broad grassy path to **Skelgill**, then join a small road where you maintain the same direction and walk a further 500 metres with the lower slopes of Cat Bells to your right, until you reach another road at a hairpin bend. ◀

Accommodation and refreshments are available at Swinside, 1km to the left on the road.

Turn left, pass over a cattle grid, then turn right through a gate and into woods, signed to Hawes End Jetty (100 metres off route; a stop for the Keswick Launch) and Portinscale. Walk across an open grassy area, always following signs for the Derwent Water Walk – and the Cumbria Way is also often signed.

This road can often feel quite busy, so take care.

After 1.5km from the cattle grid, the path eventually joins another road, with a café signed to the right. ◀ If taking the Keswick Launch from Nichol End, descend to the lake shore and the Marine. Otherwise, continue on the road into **Portinscale**. On entering the village, note the Chalet Tearooms and Restaurant on the left, then turn right, passing the Derwentwater Hotel, and continue on a path over an elegant metal bridge crossing the **River Derwent**. Keep right onto a path across fields, heading east towards the centre of Keswick. This final path emerges to cross another bridge where you turn right and walk straight into **Keswick**, and into the Market Square with the Moot Hall in the centre (16km, **4hr 50min**).

Keswick is the main market town in the northern end of the national park, and is beautifully situated with a backdrop of Skiddaw behind, and Derwent Water to the south. There is a full selection of facilities here, together with bus transport links to Penrith, the west coast, and Kendal and Windermere.

The original **Moot Hall** building was a medieval court house, but in 1570 it was leased to provide weighing and storage facilities for copper,

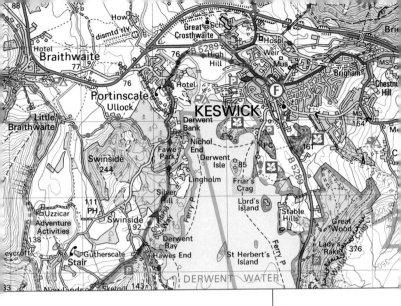

which was a thriving industry, especially in the 16th and 17th centuries when Keswick had several furnaces and a large copper smelter. The current building was constructed in 1813 to house a museum of natural history and local artefacts, but it now houses the tourist information centre downstairs, and a gallery upstairs. At the very heart of Keswick, the Moot Hall is the official start and finish point for the Bob Graham Round – a 66-mile fell-running challenge requiring the ascent of a specified 42 fell summits within 24 hours.

STAGE 5A

Buttermere to Keswick: high-level route

Start	Bridge Hotel, Buttermere
Finish	Moot Hall, Keswick
Distance	17.5km (11 miles)
Total ascent	1020m
Total descent	1050m
Time	7hr
High point	Crag Hill, 839m
Refreshments	Swinside (1km off route), Nichol End, Portinscale
Transport	Summer bus service 77/77A from Buttermere to Keswick via Honister and Rosthwaite; Keswick Launch (Derwent Water) from Hawes End and Nichol End to Keswick
Accommodation	B&B (inn) at Swinside (1km off route); hotel and B&Bs at Portinscale; all facilities at Keswick

This is a brilliant route to do on a good day, and one of the best ridge routes in the western Lake District. The climb to Whiteless Pike is steady, with ever-increasing views behind towards Hay Stacks, Red Pike, and the now distant Sca Fells and Great Gable. From the summit an elegant ridge stretches away to the north, as you begin the first of a series of roller-coaster descents and ascents to summit Crag Hill (optionally via Wandope), Sail, Scar Crags and Causey Pike. The initial descent off Causey Pike is an easy scramble, but this can be avoided. A choice of paths then leads easily down to join the low-level route in the Newlands Valley just above Rowling End Farm.

An option to save tired legs would be to take the Keswick Launch from Hawes End or Nichol End Marine to Keswick, saving around 2–4km (except in winter – see Appendix A for contact details).

With your back to the Bridge Hotel in **Buttermere**, walk up the hill to your left for 200 metres and take the path to the right opposite Crag House Farm. Immediately past

Map continues on page 96

the farm, turn right and take the right-hand path running behind a line of cottages. Pass through a gate, following the path that keeps close to a fence and later a wall.

At the point where the path begins to curve away from the fence, it splits to give a choice of three paths. (Note that the entire hillside is covered with a network of paths, many of which are not shown on the map; the green paths shown on the 1:25,000 map are merely an approximation of what is on the ground!) Take the middle

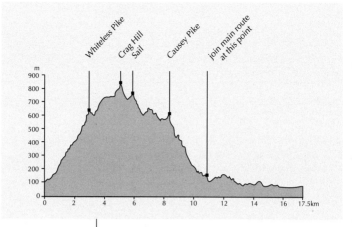

path ahead, which skirts to the right of the first prominent rocky outcrop. This leads directly and steeply up to 220m. Fork right and continue to climb with **Whiteless Breast** directly ahead.

At 285m, at a junction of several paths just below the eastern crag of Whiteless Breast (1.2km, **35min**), continue straight ahead and climb steeply in zigzags. The path then heads in a westerly direction across the flank of Whiteless Breast, drops 35m then rises again, now towards Whiteless Pike.

The route now heads straight up the side of **Whiteless Pike** on a good, clear, sometimes stone-pitched path, and after a short rocky section reaches the summit at 660m (2.9km, **1hr 40min**).

> **Views** from this first summit of the day are extensive. To the north-east the elegant Whiteless Edge leads the eye towards Crag Hill and Causey Pike. To the south-east is Fleetwith Pike and Hay Stacks, with the Sca Fell range in the distance. The ridge separating Buttermere from Ennerdale is to the south – Red Pike and High Stile dominating – then Crummock Water and Loweswater lead towards the

Irish Sea, and on a clear day the Isle of Man can be seen resting on the horizon. Finally, the great bulk of Grasmoor rises from Crummock Water to dominate the view to the north.

On Whiteless Edge, looking back at the shapely profile of Whiteless Pike

Descend to follow the ridge, heading roughly north-east, then climb again to a height of 710m and branch right. At the next path junction, 3.9km from the start of the stage, continue ahead on a small level path across the rough grass of Wandope Moss (which is actually dry and not boggy as the name might suggest) to join a wide path again heading north-east, and follow a series of large cairns to the summit of **Crag Hill** (839m) (5.1km, **3hr**).

The **views from Crag Hill** now reveal Bassenthwaite, Skiddaw and Blencathra, with Keswick and Derwent Water nestling below. The panorama of the western and northern fells is spectacular; it's hard to decide on the best view!

To climb Wandope
At the path junction at 3.9km, if you want to add another summit to your collection, the main track to the

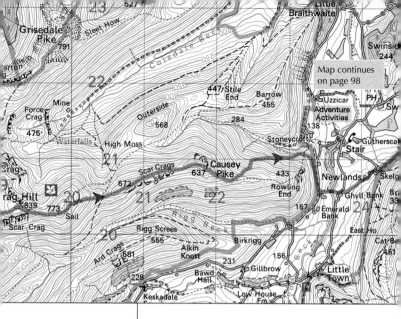

right leads directly to the summit of **Wandope** (772m), from which a path then leads north around the rim of Addacomb Hole to join with the main summit track up to **Crag Hill**.

From the summit cairn on Crag Hill, walk 50 metres in a south-easterly direction to pick up cairns that lead to the beginning of the steep descent down 'The Scar'. Although steep, this is not difficult, and you soon begin the short climb up to **Sail** summit (773m) (5.8km, **3hr 25min**). From there a restored path makes a serpentine descent to 620m and a junction of paths (6.7km, **3hr 45min**), where you have a choice of routes.

To omit Causey Pike
To avoid Causey Pike and the scramble below the summit, and for a quicker and easier descent, turn left at this point and follow the broad path across **High Moss** and down Stoneycroft Gill, and then a choice of paths can take you either to **Braithwaite** and on to **Keswick**,

or via **Stair** and **Skelgill** to join with the main route into **Keswick**. There is also a path to the left leading down just at the base of the final climb to the summit of Causey Pike, which is useful if you look at the descent from the summit and decide not to do it.

To continue on the main route, take the path directly ahead, which leads to **Scar Crags** and then on to **Causey Pike** (637m) (8.4km, **4hr 30min**). Scramble down from the summit, taking particular care in wet weather. The gradient gradually eases as you reach Sleet Hause at 470m, and a choice of paths.

Turn left on a path by a cairn and descend steadily around the north side of **Rowling End**, down stone steps, then take a right fork just before the bottom to curve around Rowling End's eastern buttress (Ellas Crag) onto a lovely contouring path which joins the Newlands road just above Rowling End Farm (11km, **5hr 45min**). Turn right and walk up the road for 50 metres, then cross the road and take the path signed to **Ghyll Bank**. ▶

The high-level and low-level routes unite on this path.

Looking back along the ridge from Causey Pike; the valley to the left is the lower-level Stage 5 route

Descend to cross Newlands Beck on a bridge, then climb through a boggy field to **Ghyll Bank**. Turn left on the road then almost immediately right over a stile in a wall to follow the broad grassy path to **Skelgill**, then join a small road where you maintain the same direction and walk a further 500 metres with the lower slopes of Cat Bells to your right, until you reach another road at a hairpin bend. ◀

Accommodation and refreshments are available at Swinside, 1km to the left on the road.

Turn left, pass over a cattle grid, then turn right through a gate and into woods, signed to Hawes End Jetty (100 metres off route; a stop for the Keswick Launch) and Portinscale. Walk across an open grassy area, always following signs for the Derwent Water Walk – and the Cumbria Way is also often signed.

This road can often feel quite busy, so take care.

After 1.5km from the cattle grid, the path eventually joins another road, with a café signed to the right. ◀ If

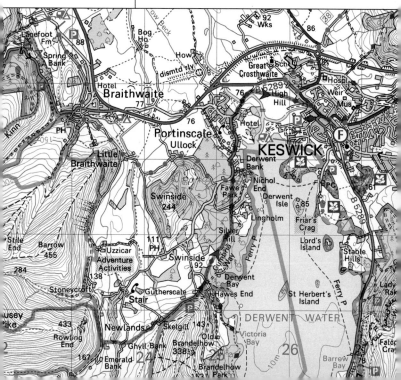

taking the Keswick Launch from Nichol End, descend to the lake shore and the Marine. Otherwise, continue on the road into **Portinscale**. On entering the village, note the Chalet Tearooms and Restaurant on the left, then turn right, passing the Derwentwater Hotel, and continue on a path over an elegant metal bridge crossing the **River Derwent**. Keep right onto a path across fields, heading east towards the centre of Keswick. This final path emerges to cross another bridge where you turn right and walk straight into **Keswick**, and into the Market Square with the Moot Hall in the centre (17.5km, **7hr**).

> **Keswick** is the main market town in the northern end of the national park, and is beautifully situated with a backdrop of Skiddaw behind, and Derwent Water to the south. There is a full selection of facilities here, together with bus transport links to Penrith, the west coast, and Kendal and Windermere.
>
> The original **Moot Hall** building was a medieval court house, but in 1570 it was leased to provide weighing and storage facilities for copper, which was a thriving industry, especially in the 16th and 17th centuries when Keswick had several furnaces and a large copper smelter. The current building was constructed in 1813 to house a museum of natural history and local artefacts, but it now houses the tourist information centre downstairs, and a gallery upstairs. At the very heart of Keswick, the Moot Hall is the official start and finish point for the Bob Graham Round – a 66-mile fell-running challenge requiring the ascent of a specified 42 fell summits within 24 hours.

STAGE 6
Keswick to Rosthwaite

Start	Moot Hall, Keswick
Finish	Rosthwaite
Distance	15.5km (9½ miles)
Total ascent	560m
Total descent	560m
Time	5hr
High point	Walla Crag, 376m
Refreshments	Watendlath (National Trust tearoom), Rosthwaite
Transport	78 bus from Keswick to Rosthwaite
Accommodation	Hotels, B&B, hostel and camping at (or near) Rosthwaite; other options available elsewhere in the Borrowdale valley

This is a stage to be relished, with numerous highlights along the way. The highly atmospheric Castlerigg Stone Circle is reached within the first hour, then the Tour heads across farmland to climb to the summit of Walla Crag, with extensive views in all directions. A good broad path descends gently across the fells to the pretty packhorse bridge at Ashness. From here you climb again through Ashness Wood before entering a beautiful and 'hidden' valley, following a stream up to the tiny community of Watendlath. A short, steep final climb brings you to a broad and remote moorland before you descend into the Borrowdale valley at Rosthwaite.

In bad weather and poor visibility a low-level alternative route might be preferred: from Keswick, partly retrace the final 3–4km of Stage 5, then follow the waymarked Cumbria Way along the west side of Derwent Water to Grange, then on to Rosthwaite. This 13km route is likely to take 3hr to 3hr 30min.

Note: Rosthwaite is a stage on the Cumbria Way and the Coast to Coast route, so finding accommodation may be difficult. A regular bus service to Keswick (25min) provides easy access to many more accommodation options.

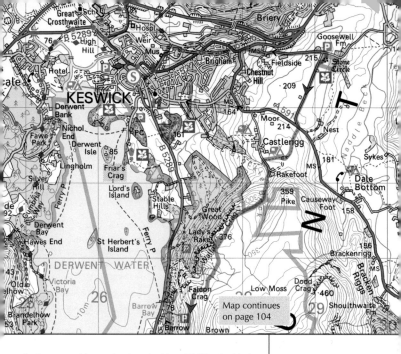

Map continues on page 104

Facing east with your back to the Moot Hall in the Market Square in **Keswick**, walk up Station Street, then turn left (still on Station Street) and on meeting the Penrith Road cross straight over, with gardens on the right, passing the YHA hostel and sports fields on the left. The road bends

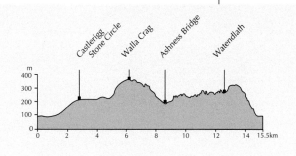

The original Keswick station building is seen on the right.

to the right but keep straight ahead, signed for the C2C cycle route.

Pass to the right of Keswick Leisure Pool, then turn right to begin an easy walk along the old railway path. ◄ This is a traffic-free route out of Keswick, but watch out for bicycles, as the path is shared with the C2C cycle route. After a little over 1.3km from the Moot Hall, leave the railway path opposite the last house on the left on a smaller path rising to the right. At the main road, cross carefully, continue uphill then turn left then immediately right onto a small road signed to Castlerigg Stone Circle (1.4km, **20min**).

This small road climbs steeply and steadily with emerging views of the northern fells. Although generally quiet, especially first thing in the morning, it can be busy at other times as it is the only access road for traffic visiting the stone circle directly from Keswick. Eventually the gradient eases to reach a series of gates on the right into a field where you'll find **Castlerigg Stone Circle** (3km, **50min**).

CASTLERIGG STONE CIRCLE

The exceptionally beautiful setting of Castlerigg Stone Circle

Our ancestors who constructed Castlerigg Stone Circle around 4–5000 years ago certainly chose an incredibly atmospheric setting. Emerging onto an unexpected elevated plateau after the climb out from Keswick, you see the stones standing proudly with commanding views in all directions. Meaning 'The fort on the ridge' in Old English, the circle predates Stonehenge. As it predates the emergence of the Druids, it is thought that it was used as an assembly point for local tribes for ritualistic and religious ceremonies, and as a regional marketplace. Many of the stones stand around 2m above the ground, arranged in a near-perfect circle of about 30m in diameter. Currently it consists of 38 stones, although originally there were 42.

Skiddaw, Blencathra and the northern fells dominate the scene. Further to the south-east is the distinctive wedge of Helvellyn, and south are the fells you will soon cross – Walla Crag, with Bleaberry Fell and High Seat just to the left – and then the fells of the western Lake District, with Maiden Moor in the foreground, dwarfed by the giants behind (including Scafell Pike on a clear day), far in the distance.

Facing south, head for the far-right corner of the field and climb over the stone stile, then turn left to walk down Castle Lane and reach the busy **A591** road. Cross the road quickly and with care. This is the main road between Grasmere and Keswick. It may be necessary to walk slightly up or down the road to gain better visibility. Now follow the continuing footpath, keeping to the right-hand side of fields, and pass through two gates before turning sharp right at a third gate. The track soon swings left, but keep ahead through another gate, then right to follow an ancient path next to a wall. ▶

Castlerigg Farm campsite is behind the wall.

On meeting a lane, turn left, then bear right at **Rakefoot Farm**. Cross the footbridge over **Brockle Beck** and begin climbing towards Walla Crag. The well-used path climbs steeply, then eases a little to join a stone wall on the right. (A small gap in the wall leads to an exposed rocky path, which can be slippery when wet, undulating at the edge of the crag leading directly to the summit. **Avoid this path.**) Continue with the wall on the right then go through a gate to reach the summit of **Walla Crag** (376m) (6.2km, **2hr**).

Views from this modest height encompass a panorama of the western and northern fells, with Derwent Water glistening below, Keswick nestling just above its northern shore, and Bassenthwaite Lake stretching into the distance, wedged just to the west of the great bulk of Skiddaw.

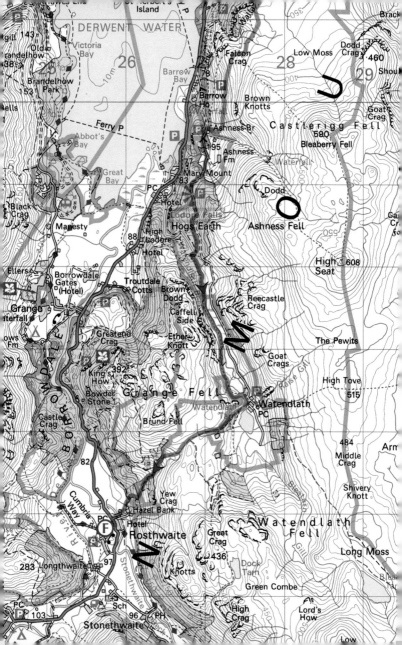

From the summit, take the path heading south to cross over a stile, then turn right and drop a few metres before forking left away from the fence. This broad and easy path now contours across the flank of **Low Moss**, enjoying constant views to the western fells and Derwent Water below. After just over 1km, descend on the path to pass through a gate, then cross Barrow Beck to join a path between the stream and a wall and follow this down to **Ashness Bridge** (8.5km, **2hr 45min**).

After enjoying the views from this much-photographed packhorse bridge, turn south to walk up the road, passing **Ashness Farm** (B&B). After about 1km, pass a **car park** just above Lodore Wood, with more superb views, then exactly 1.2km from Ashness Bridge the path levels out. Leave the road here to fork right on a broad woodland path signed 'Watendlath 1½ miles'. ▶

Pass through a gate at the far end of the woods and turn right. Cross a bridge then turn left, maintaining a

Ashness Bridge, spanning pretty Barrow Beck, is a popular beauty spot

These beautiful woods are predominantly made up of oak, known as Atlantic oakwoods, and are designated as a Special Area of Conservation.

Watendlath Beck and Tarn, with the bridleway leading over Puddlestone Bank

The name Watendlath is derived from the Norse, and probably means 'the land [or the barn] at the end of the lake'.

southerly direction, and follow **Watendlath Beck**. A peaceful valley stretches ahead, with the path keeping close to the stream. The path is quite stony for most of the way; turning left to use the road rather than turning right after passing through the gate at the end of the woodland path as described above would be about 15min quicker. Towards the far end of the valley, climb stone steps to a gate, then continue for a further kilometre to arrive at the isolated and picturesque hamlet of **Watendlath** and its attractive tarn (12.6km, **3hr 45min**). ◄

Cross the tiny packhorse bridge to enter the hamlet and explore. Return over the packhorse bridge and, with the river and tarn on your left, take the path south, then fork right up a steep old drove road. The route soon levels out at about 330m to cross a high moorland on a good path, then begins to descend. Keep ahead at a path junction and gate just below the 'resting stone', then pass through a gate onto a track.

Continue to descend on this stony track, then turn right through a gate, following signs to Rosthwaite. At the bottom of the hill turn right to cross over **Stonethwaite Beck**, then turn left on the main road to enter the village of **Rosthwaite** (15.5km, **4hr 40min**).

Rosthwaite, 'the clearing with the cairn', is a small, pretty village with hotels and a tearoom. A hostel and two campsites are within 1km.

STAGE 7
Rosthwaite to Grasmere

Start	Royal Oak Hotel, Rosthwaite
Finish	Grasmere
Distance	14km (8 miles)
Total ascent	580m
Total descent	600m
Time	5hr
High point	Greenup Edge, 610m
Transport	555 bus from Grasmere to Keswick and Ambleside/ Windermere
Accommodation	All facilities at Grasmere. There is no accommodation of any kind between Rosthwaite and Grasmere.

On this stage you leave the flat valley floor of Borrowdale and once again climb high into the fells, this time exploring those which separate Borrowdale from Easedale. The climb is steady, with a short steep section up Lining Crag leading to Greenup Edge, where a number of paths diverge. This high, open moorland provides excellent views but in poor visibility can be a confusing place where good navigation skills are needed. It can be quite boggy at times, before a thankfully drier path descends into the valley of Far Easedale. As you draw nearer to Grasmere the path broadens, forming part of a popular circular walk from Grasmere to Easedale Tarn.

If you need to cut your Tour short, there's the option of walking directly to Ambleside from Grasmere, thereby omitting the last two days of the main route. This option is detailed below.

With your back to the Royal Oak Hotel in **Rosthwaite**, turn right (north) and walk along the road for 50 metres, then turn right onto a bridleway sighed to Stonethwaite and Watendlath. Cross the bridge over **Stonethwaite Beck** then turn right onto an enclosed stony path, (known as an 'outgang', used to confine sheep when moving them from one location to another) which leads in just over 1km to a turning to **Stonethwaite bridge**. ▶

Stonethwaite is an unspoilt farming hamlet, with a pub (food and accommodation) and campsite.

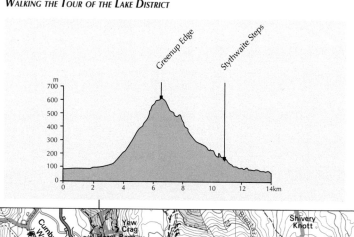

Map continues on page 111

Do not cross the bridge; instead keep ahead, and after passing through a series of gates come to a path junction. The right-hand path crosses the beck and enters Langstrath. Ignore this and continue ahead on the path rising steadily, keeping parallel with Stonethwaite Beck. The valley begins to narrow a little, and on passing through a gate in the fell wall (250m) you begin to enter the upper section of the valley. Greenup Gill is to the right, and there are broadening views south towards the Sca Fell range. Continue to climb, more steeply now, to reach a rise at 395m (5km, **2hr**).

The pretty Stonethwaite Beck, looking towards Stonethwaite and the fells

Ahead the steep face of Lining Crag begins to dominate, but this short steep climb is easily achieved on the well-made stone-pitched path (slippery in wet conditions) and after 10–15min on this steeper gradient, gentler grassy slopes open up, leading towards Greenup Edge. In poor visibility this is a bleak place, often very wet underfoot as you traverse peaty bogs and tussocks, but the path is well used and there are several cairns indicating the way.

The ridgeline of **Greenup Edge** (610m) is reached (6.6km, **2hr 45min**), with an old parish boundary marked by decaying iron fence posts. The route now

Looking down the Greenup Gill valley, with Borrowdale seen far below

takes the descending path ahead in an easterly direction, with other paths leading either north-east and down to Wythburn, or up to High Raise in a south-westerly direction. Be sure to take the correct path (especially in poor visibility), otherwise you'll end up in the wrong valley!

Continue towards some low crags over more boggy ground, crossing and recrossing a stream. Eventually the path rises again to reach the crest of the Far Easedale valley (480m), marked by fence posts, with good views ahead (7.8km, **3hr 30min**). From here on there is no more climbing to be done, and as the path descends it follows the course of **Far Easedale Gill**, and Helm Crag (known affectionately as 'the Lion and the Lamb') comes into view.

At Stythwaite Steps a path from Easedale Tarn joins from the right. Continue ahead, cross the stream on the footbridge and (now with the stream on your right) continue steadily down. The path broadens to become a track running between drystone walls. Pass a few houses at **Lancrigg** and continue onto Easedale Road, which leads directly into **Grasmere** (14km, **5hr**).

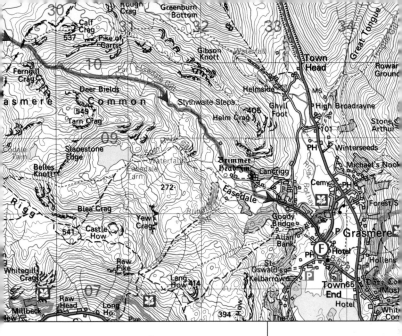

Grasmere, as the name suggests, is the 'lake with grassy shores'. The oversized village has been a favourite destination for walkers and visitors from around the world for many years.

Dove Cottage was the home of **William Wordsworth** between 1799 and 1808, and while the cottage remains in its original condition, the superb museum next door displays manuscripts and other items belonging to Wordsworth. Wordsworth also lived at Rydal Mount, a 2–3km walk to the south-east of Dove Cottage. This was his final home from 1813 until his death in 1850. Rydal Mount and its gardens are open to the public daily but have limited opening hours between November and March, and the house is closed for maintenance in January.

While you're in Grasmere, don't miss the Heaton Cooper Studio with its fantastic selection of watercolour prints of the Lake District, and if you like gingerbread, make a beeline for the Grasmere Gingerbread Shop in the south of the village.

Alternative finish (saving two days of walking): 8km, 2hr

If time is short, from Grasmere follow Red Bank Road from the south-west of the village (opposite the parish church). Follow this for about 1.6km then take a footpath branching off to the left immediately before the road begins to rise steeply. Either follow the delightful lower lakeside path, or immediately take the right-hand path to climb about 60m onto the Loughrigg Terrace path around the southern shores of Grasmere with fine views of the two lakes and the surrounding fells. Both paths join at a height of 100m, then wander gently at the foot of Loughrigg on the southern shore of Rydal Water to reach a road at Pelter Bridge just to the south of Rydal and Rydal Mount. From here turn right on a narrow road, first across pastures with the River Rothay on your left, then continue on this minor road for 2km to reach Ambleside.

The path picks its way down beautiful Far Easedale, with Helm Crag seen in the middle distance

STAGE 8

Grasmere to Patterdale

Start	Grasmere
Finish	Patterdale
Distance	13km (8 miles)
Total ascent	610m
Total descent	530m
Time	4hr
High point	Grisedale Hause, 590m
Refreshments	Travellers Rest pub (200 metres from route) outside Grasmere; various in Patterdale
Accommodation	Camping, youth hostels, B&Bs and hotels at Patterdale and Glenridding; camping at Brothers Water (into Stage 9)

This stage is one of the shorter stages of the Tour, allowing ample time to explore Grasmere before the walk over to Patterdale. However, if the weather is fine and you have the energy, then choosing the longer high-level route over Helvellyn (Stage 8A) might be preferred.

The route out of Grasmere is initially dominated by the view of iconic Helm Crag as you follow quiet narrow lanes which meander easily through farmland. The views expand to the north and east as the busy A591 crossing is approached. From here a bridleway leads up into the fells, with the steep craggy side of Seat Sandal to the left, and the slopes of Great Rigg and Fairfield rising to the right. The grassy path is always clear as height is gained, sometimes steeply, with superb views behind you back into the valley. On reaching Grisedale Hause, the highest point, the tarn below seems dwarfed by the surrounding high fells. The descent through Grisedale is steep and rocky at first, but the path is always clear and good. The gradient eases as lower slopes are reached, passing the tiny Ruthwaite Lodge, then descending further to reach farm lanes, and eventually Patterdale.

Beginning in the centre of **Grasmere**, with your back to the Sam Read bookshop, cross the main road onto Easedale Road, signed to Easedale Tarn. After a few

Map continues on page 116

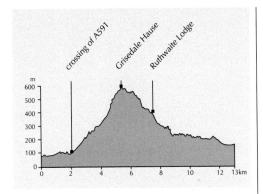

minutes, pass the youth hostel (right), with Helm Crag ('the Lion and the Lamb') seen ahead of you. Pass a series of cottages (right), then cross a bridge past 'Goody Rise' and turn right (700 metres, **8min**).

The road now rises and is joined by a lane on the left at Thorney How. Continue on the road past Underhelm Farm with views towards Fairfield on the right and Helvellyn and Dunmail Pass ahead. At a junction of lanes, turn right over a bridge and walk up to the main road (2km, **25min**). ▶

Cross straight over the main road (**A591**) and continue immediately ahead on the bridleway signed to Patterdale. Climb steadily with increasing views towards Dunmail, with Helm Crag now behind you. The ancient path is cobbled in places, rising steadily before levelling as you pass through a gate, then cross a stream. There is a choice of paths here, each one passing either side of the great mound of **Great Tongue** seen directly ahead (2.8km, **45min**).

The best path is the one to the right, which is well maintained. This is also used for the Coast to Coast long-distance route. Cross another stream and begin to climb steadily, with **Tongue Gill** and a wall to your left. Several tributary streams are crossed as the path steadily rises, becoming steeper as the head of the valley and waterfalls are approached. The alternative path now joins from the

For refreshments at the Travellers Rest Inn, take the path on the right immediately after crossing the bridge. The path leads across fields directly to the pub.

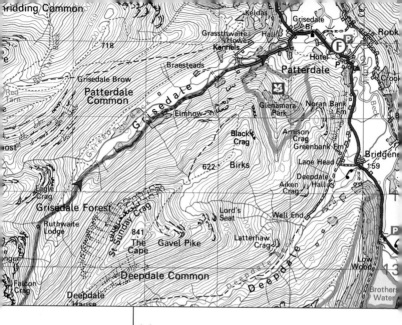

left. Continue ahead with the path now climbing more steeply, crossing an old section of scree. The final section is on a pitched path to **Grisedale Hause** (Hause Gap) at 590m, with Grisedale Tarn just below and ahead (5.9km, **2hr**).

Grisedale Tarn is surrounded by a number of imposing fells – Seat Sandal, Dollywaggon Pike, St Sunday Crag and Fairfield looming above. It's a wild, desolate place, and it's rare to be able to consider paddling in the water, except on the hottest summer days.

It is thought that in AD945–6, the 'last king of Cumbria' – King Dunmail – was defeated in battle by the West Saxon English king, Edmund. Legend has it that this battle took place on what is now known as Dunmail Raise, where a huge pile of stones is said to mark the spot where Dunmail fell and is buried – although it may be that it more significantly marks the boundary between the ancient

Scottish border with England, or the old boundary between Cumberland and Westmoreland. Legend further describes how Dunmail's followers escaped into the mountains and threw Dunmail's crown into Grisedale Tarn, so preserving its safety 'til Dunmail come again to lead us'.

Descend towards the tarn and continue on the path above the southern shore to the far end, then cross over the outflow on rough stepping-stones. After a further minute come to a junction of paths by a large pile of stones. These provide welcome shelter in windy conditions, and make a good spot for a snack before beginning the descent.

Continue in a north-north-easterly direction, now downhill. The path is initially steep and stony as it threads its way, keeping to the left side of the valley below Dollywaggon Pike. About 2km from the tarn, pass the tiny **Ruthwaite Lodge**. ▶

Grisedale Tarn is often wild and windy and is surrounded by dramatic fells

Built on the site of an old mine in 1854, this climbing hut has been restored on two occasions, most recently by the Outward Bound in 1990.

Superb views from Ruthwaite Lodge down into Grisedale

Below the lodge, keep right at the first footbridge, then cross **Grisedale Beck** shortly afterwards on another footbridge. The gradient finally eases as the valley floor is reached and the path becomes a track. Continue down the track, keeping to the right-hand side of the stream and valley until the track eventually joins a small metalled road, which then drops to reach the main road at **Grisedale Bridge** opposite the Patterdale Mountain Rescue Centre. Turn right and walk the final 500 metres along the road into Patterdale (13km, **4hr**).

Patterdale and neighbouring **Glenridding** lie at the southern end of Ullswater and between them provide all services, including a tourist information centre at Glenridding. Steamers ply up and down the lake, bringing visitors in some numbers during the summer months. Patterdale ('Patrick's valley') and Glenridding ('The valley full of bracken'), their names derived from Gaelic origins, are the main access points from which most people climb Helvellyn, especially via the ever-popular (but difficult) Striding Edge and the marginally easier Swirral Edge routes.

STAGE 8A

Grasmere to Patterdale: high-level route

Start	Grasmere
Finish	Patterdale
Distance	16km (10 miles); or 19.5km (12 miles) via Glenridding Common
Total ascent	1100m
Total descent	1020m
Time	6hr; or 6hr 30min via Glenridding Common
High point	Helvellyn, 950m
Refreshments	Travellers Rest pub (200 metres from route) outside Grasmere; various in Patterdale
Accommodation	Camping, youth hostels, B&Bs and hotels at Patterdale and Glenridding; camping at Brothers Water (into Stage 9)

This stage traverses Helvellyn, the third highest and one of the best mountains in the Lake District, with fine views in all directions. Paths are good, so although there is a fair amount of ascent in the stage, it is fairly easy walking throughout, dry under foot and with no difficulties. There are several descent options from Helvellyn, including those for the more experienced walker (down the 'edges' to Glenridding and Patterdale), and a longer route more suitable for backpackers.

The first two hours of the stage, from Grasmere to Grisedale Hause between Seat Sandal and Fairfield, are shared with the lower-level Stage 8.

Note: The Striding Edge option should only be taken by experienced walkers, ideally having done the route before. Not only is it very exposed, but when descending you may still be going against the 'flow' of walkers on the edge using it as an ascent route, with consequent difficulties in passing safely. If you are not experienced, or are loaded with backpacking gear, then you are strongly advised to take the longer route described. Striding Edge is much 'edgier' than Swirral Edge, but if wet or if there is snow or ice around then both should be avoided.

Map continues
on page 123

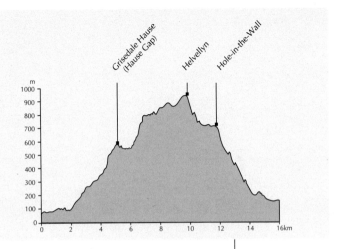

Beginning in the centre of **Grasmere**, with your back to the Sam Read bookshop, cross the main road onto Easedale Road, signed to Easedale Tarn. After a few minutes, pass the youth hostel (right), with Helm Crag ('the Lion and the Lamb') seen ahead of you. Pass a series of cottages (right), then cross a bridge past 'Goody Rise' and turn right (700 metres, **8min**).

The road now rises and is joined by a lane on the left at Thorney How. Continue on the road past Underhelm Farm with views towards Fairfield on the right and Helvellyn and Dunmail Pass ahead. At a junction of lanes, turn right over a bridge and walk up to the main road (2km, **25min**).

Cross straight over the main road (**A591**) and continue immediately ahead on the bridleway signed to Patterdale. Climb steadily with increasing views towards Dunmail, with Helm Crag now behind you. The ancient path is cobbled in places, rising steadily before levelling as you pass through a gate, then cross a stream. There is a choice of paths here, each one passing either side of the great mound of **Great Tongue** seen directly ahead (2.8km, **45min**).

Approaching the steeper section of the Tongue Gill path

Fairfield and Seat Sandal can both be easily climbed from this point, adding 1hr and 30min, respectively, for the round trips.

The best path is the one to the right, which is well maintained. This is also used for the Coast to Coast long-distance route. Cross another stream and begin to climb steadily, with **Tongue Gill** and a wall to your left. Several tributary streams are crossed as the path steadily rises, becoming steeper as the head of the valley and waterfalls are approached. The alternative path now joins from the left. Continue ahead with the path now climbing more steeply, crossing an old section of scree. The final section is on a pitched path to **Grisedale Hause** (Hause Gap) at 590m, with Grisedale Tarn just below and ahead (5.9km, **2hr**). ◀

Grisedale Tarn is surrounded by a number of imposing fells – Seat Sandal, Dollywaggon Pike, St Sunday Crag and Fairfield looming above. It's a wild, desolate place, and it's rare to be able to consider paddling in the water, except on the hottest summer days.

It is thought that in AD945–6, the 'last king of Cumbria' – King Dunmail – was defeated in battle by the West Saxon English king, Edmund. Legend has it that this battle took place on what is now known as Dunmail Raise, where a huge pile of stones is said to mark the spot where Dunmail fell and is buried – although it may be that it more significantly marks the boundary between the ancient Scottish border with England, or the old boundary between Cumberland and Westmoreland. Legend further describes how Dunmail's followers escaped into the mountains and threw Dunmail's crown into Grisedale Tarn, so preserving its safety "til Dunmail come again to lead us'.

Take the path down and right to pass to the east of **Grisedale Tarn**. After crossing its outflow, find a substantial cairn and turn left to begin the graded ascent of Dollywaggon Pike. This is a good path and height is quickly gained. Once on the shoulder of the mountain there is a choice: either stay on the main path that passes under the summits of **Dollywaggon Pike** and **Nethermost Pike** directly to Helvellyn, or head right and take in the peaks with views over the substantial cliffs to the east. Whichever option you choose, the paths reunite before the final easy gradient to the summit of

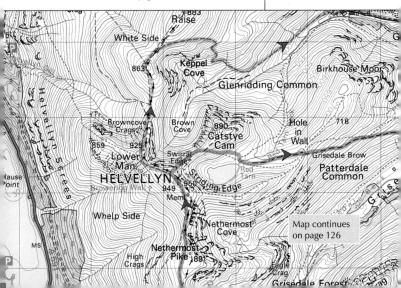

Map continues on page 126

In very windy conditions the more direct route keeping away from the impressive cliffs is recommended.

Helvellyn. ◀ Climb easily to the summit of **Helvellyn** (950m) (9.9km, **3hr 45min**). The summit has a substantial shelter. You are unlikely to have this to yourself!

Every winter, between December and March, three **fell-top assessors** take turns to climb to the summit of Helvellyn to report weather and snow conditions, and take photographs. This information is fed back to the Met Office and is reported on Weatherline, the Lake District National Park's weather forecasting service. The reports help to ensure the safety of climbers and walkers, providing up-to-date information on snow, ice and avalanche status.

There are three possible onward routes from Helvellyn: down Swirral Edge (the main route); the longer but easier descent by Glenridding Common and Glenridding Beck; or down Striding Edge (the hardest route – for experienced walkers only).

For the main route, from the summit, continue north for 200 metres and find the top of the ridge by a large cairn. The initial 60m descent is very steep, with exposure, then the way eases slightly. Fork right to begin a more steady descent with **Red Tarn** seen below, and at a path junction above the eastern end of the tarn bear right, and continue ahead. A right fork drops to the eastern shore of Red Tarn. The path now continues more steadily to reach Hole-in-the-Wall (710m) (11.8km, **5hr**).

Pass over a stile, then maintain direction to continue the long, steady descent, eventually reaching a fell wall and gate, with a group of buildings (kennels) seen in the valley. Pass through the gate and cross the valley to the right of the **kennels**, then turn left onto the small road which leads directly down to reach the main Patterdale road. Turn right to walk into **Patterdale** (16km, **6hr**) or left to Glenridding, 1.5km (20min) along the road.

Striding Edge

From the summit of Helvellyn, head south-east towards two cairns for 100 metres and take the narrow ridge

down. The Striding Edge and Swirral Edge routes converge at Hole-in-the-Wall; from there, continue as described above.

Descending the difficult section of Swirral Edge

Via Glenridding Common

For the Glenridding route, from the summit of Helvellyn continue north-west along the rim above cliffs. The path keeps a little way to the left. Pass a substantial cairn marking the top of **Swirral Edge**, continue for a further 500 metres and turn right at **Lower Man**. Descend a broad ridge and then climb to **White Side**, and shortly afterwards come to a right turn (822m), about 45min after the summit of Helvellyn (12km, **4hr 30min**).

Turn right down the hill. Initially the path is level but it soon drops steeply down a well-made zigzagged path, joins with a track and continues steadily down. Above a weir over the Glenridding Beck, keep left to pass close by holiday accommodation and then a **youth hostel**. ▶ After the hostel the track steadily improves and gains a partial veneer of tarmac. Passing cottages, it drops past the

At the weir there is an option to cross to the south of the stream and take higher cross-country paths to Patterdale.

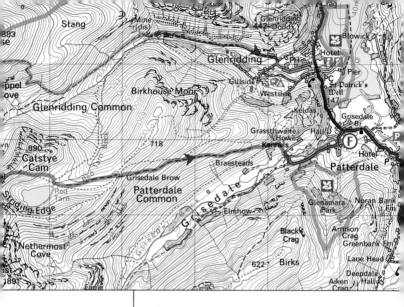

Travellers Rest pub and then a small road leads into the village of **Glenridding** (18km, **6hr**). Continue south along the road on a good footway to reach **Patterdale** (19.5km, **6hr 20min**).

> **Patterdale** and neighbouring **Glenridding** lie at the southern end of Ullswater and between them provide all services, including a tourist information centre at Glenridding. Steamers ply up and down the lake, bringing visitors in some numbers during the summer months. Patterdale ('Patrick's valley') and Glenridding ('The valley full of bracken'), their names derived from Gaelic origins, are the main access points from which most people climb Helvellyn.

STAGE 9

Patterdale to Ambleside

Start	Patterdale Hotel, Patterdale
Finish	Ambleside
Distance	18km (11 miles) via Red Screes; 15km (9½ miles) via alternative direct route
Total ascent	750m
Total descent	840m
Time	5–6hr; 4hr 15min via direct route
High point	Red Screes, 776m (or Scandale Pass, 520m)
Refreshments	Brotherswater Inn (off route)
Accommodation	Camping at Brothers Water

This stage provides a delightful final day of traversing the fells. While the lower route is a perfect mix of pastoral, lakeside and fell walking, the higher route via Red Screes makes a fitting finale to the Tour. It is the preferred route, with exceptional 360-degree views from the summit of Red Screes on a good clear day. The way from Patterdale begins with mostly level valley walking, with views towards Kirkstone Pass and the high fells of Fairfield and Hart Crag to the south-west. Passing to the west of Brothers Water, the route then enters Caiston Glen, rising to reach Scandale Pass. From here on a clear day you can see many of the fells and valleys visited on the Tour. The Red Screes route offers a superb (but often boggier) ridge walk to Ambleside, while the slightly shorter direct route descends to follow the valley bottom straight into Ambleside.

From the Patterdale Hotel in **Patterdale**, walk south along the road past the White Lion Inn, then take the narrow road left to cross the river. On reaching the small group of cottages turn right, signed 'Hartsop 2 miles'. The road soon becomes a track with meadows to the right and the Kirkstone Pass ahead. Pass through **Crookabeck Farm** (barn and wool shop, B&B at Crookey Cottage), then through a gate.

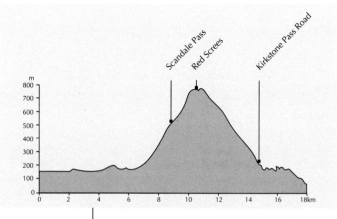

The track now becomes a path through light woods, then it passes through a metal gate at **Beckstones Farm**. Shortly after the farm, continue ahead at a left-hand fork, with a small bridge seen below to the right, then at the next fork keep right through a gate on the bridleway. ◄ Continue for just under 1km to reach a minor road, turn right, then turn right again onto the pavement next to the main A592 road. On reaching a **parking area** at Cow Bridge cross the road and turn left, with the sparkling **Brothers Water** ahead (2.8km, **45min**).

The left fork here is a path into Hartsop village.

After another 1.5km pass through a gate to reach **Hartsop Hall** (farm). Pass through a further gate and behind the farm, then swing left, then diagonally right to go through a small gate in a wall, with a prominent National Trust sign 'Footpath to Kirkstone Pass and Scandale Pass'.

Hartsop Hall is a 16th-century Grade I listed building that is one of the oldest and most important in Patterdale. Formerly home of the de Lancasters, in the 17th century it was inherited by Sir John Lowther, a member of the family that later became Earls of Lonsdale, and which remains a prominent landowner in the area. There are stories relating to

Map continues
on page 133

The lakeside path next to Brothers Water has good views towards Kirkstone Pass and Red Screes

smuggling, murder and ghosts at Hartsop Hall, and it is also believed that monks resided there, giving rise to the name 'Brothers Water'. Most of the current house is thought to be made up of additions and improvements made in the 16th century to an earlier, possibly 14th-century bastle house (a fortified farmhouse). Features in the Grade I listing include 16th-century moulded beams and part of a king-post roof, a garderobe (a medieval toilet) and a priest's hole.

Cross a large flat pasture and go over a small bridge ahead, then follow a faint grassy track across a further field full of large boulders. To the right are the formidable rocky buttresses of Dove Crag at the head of Dovedale, with the flanks of High Hartsop Dodd dominating the immediate foreground. ◄

In May and early June these hillsides are covered in bluebells.

Continue through a gate next to a barn, then, keeping the fell wall to your left, continue slightly uphill, still in a southerly direction with Kirkstone Pass ahead. After 6.8km (**1hr 30min**) from the stage start, the path begins to rise a little at grid ref NY 399 109. Notice two footbridges below and to your left; these lead to the path towards Kirkstone Pass. Instead fork slightly right, rising steeply to pass through a gate in the wall and enter **Caiston Glen**. Keep the fell wall and stream to your left as you walk up through the glen.

> **Caiston Glen** has a sense of remoteness, and the relatively easy height gain is on a good path through wildflowers and bracken, with Caiston Beck providing occasional small cascades over the rocks.

The path steepens in the upper valley to reach **Scandale Pass** at 520m (8.8km, **2hr 30min**). The views west from the pass are towards the Coniston and Langdale fells, with the pyramid outline of Harter Fell in the far distance behind Hardknott Pass.

The direct route now crosses the wall over a ladder stile and descends on an old bridleway through the valley directly to Ambleside – see alternative route description below. However, in good weather and when time allows, the recommended route climbs to Red Screes then descends along a ridge to Ambleside.

For the Red Screes option, at the top of Scandale Pass turn left and follow the fell wall, keeping it to your right. The path rises steadily, occasionally over rocky slabs and outcrops, with broadening views to the right (west) as height is gained. As the wall takes a sharp bend to the right, follow the broad path left at an easier gradient to reach the summit of **Red Screes** at 776m (10.3km, **3hr 30min**).

> From here in fine weather the **views** are exceptional. Looking south, the outline of Windermere stretches into the distance, with the Irish Sea on the horizon. Looking south-west and west you'll see the Coniston fells and the central fells visited during the previous few days, then to the north and north-west the formidable outline of Striding Edge leads to the summit of Helvellyn in the distance, with Fairfield and Dove Crag in the foreground and the Patterdale

valley far below. Looking east, a prominent distant ridgeline separates the Troutbeck and Kentdale valleys, while far below is Kirkstone Pass.

Three paths lead from the summit. To the north-west is the path that you've followed from Scandale Pass. To the south-east is a difficult, steep and exposed path which drops directly to Kirkstone Pass. The correct path heads in a south-westerly direction, passing just to the left of the tarn. This is a wonderful path, descending gently over broad grassy slopes, keeping just to the right of the crest of the ridge. In some places the ground may be quite boggy after heavy rain.

As you descend further, pass a rocky outcrop in the crest of the ridge (**Snarker Pike**, 644m) and shortly after this the path forks. Take the right-hand fork and cross over a wall, then go through a gate and after a short while cross another wall on a ladder stile at 500m (12.5km, **4hr**). To the right lies the Scandale valley, with the ridge leading up to Fairfield behind, while Rydal Water and Loughrigg are seen ahead.

It's easy to stride out along the ridge path as you descend towards Ambleside, with Windermere far below

Now the path swings south again, following to the left-hand side of a fell wall. Pass through a gate (now between two walls) and continue downhill, sometimes quite steeply, to eventually reach the **Kirkstone Pass road**.

The direct way to Ambleside is straight down this road for just over 1km; however, there is no pavement

and although there is generally little traffic, the road is steep with numerous bends, so not ideal. For a more interesting final approach, if you have time and energy, walk downhill for 300 metres to the first building on your left, then take the tarmacked bridleway forking sharply left to **Roundhill Farm**.

On reaching the farm, look for a small gate to the right of the larger farm gate seen ahead. The path leads down in a zigzag through a meadow, then parallel to the Stock Ghyll stream before crossing over a footbridge. Climb directly up through the next field to reach a small lane. Turn right to follow this delightful little road down towards Ambleside, with superb views ahead towards Loughrigg and the fells beyond, and with Wansfell above on the left.

Pass a path on the right signed to **Stockghyll Force** waterfalls (worth a short detour) before reaching the town centre of **Ambleside**, and the end of your Tour of the Lake District (18km, **6hr**).

For public transport connections, turn left and walk along the main street, passing several shops and pubs, then turn right into the market square for buses to Windermere, Keswick and onward destinations.

Alternative direct route
At Scandale Pass, climb over the stile and begin the descent on a clear but sometimes rocky path, going

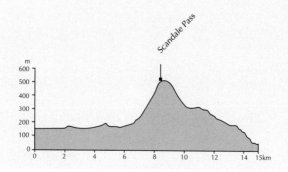

through a gate then keeping a wall on your right as the gradient eases into the upper part of Scandale ('short valley'). Follow the now grassy path, and after 1km from the pass, go through a second gate next to a large sheepfold. A track is easily followed all the way down the pretty valley, with good views ahead and occasional stream crossings which can make for a squelchy time in wet weather. After 3.3km from the pass, at about 230m, look to the right to find the pretty **High Sweden Bridge** – a lovely place to rest for a while, with a path crossing the bridge leading to the fells of Sweden Crag and Low Pike, on the eastern arm of the well-known Fairfield Horseshoe circuit. After viewing the bridge, resume on the track, passing through two gates. Follow a wall next to Sweden Wood, then go through a final gate to join a tarmac road and follow this steeply down. Turn right and continue down to reach the centre of **Ambleside**, emerging opposite a large car park (15km, **4hr 15min**).

High Sweden Bridge is a popular spot for a picnic

APPENDIX A
Useful contacts

You may find the following websites and apps useful. If you are intending to use information on your smartphone, ensure that the data – especially any mapping – is downloaded before you set off. Many parts of the Lake District have no mobile signal or wi-fi.

General information about the Lake District
Cumbria Tourism
www.visitlakedistrict.com

Lake District National Park
www.lakedistrict.gov.uk

Tourist information centres
Bowness on Windermere
Glebe Road, Bowness on Windermere
tel 0845 901 0845
email: BownessTIC@lakedistrict.gov.uk
www.lakedistrict.gov.uk/visiting/
plan-your-visit/information-centres

Ullswater (in Glenridding)
Beckside Car Park,
Glenridding
tel 0845 901 0845
email: UllswaterTIC@lakedistrict.gov.uk
www.lakedistrict.gov.uk/visiting/
plan-your-visit/information-centres

Keswick
Moot Hall, Market Square
tel 017687 72645
email: KeswickTIC@lakedistrict.gov.uk
www.lakedistrict.gov.uk/visiting/
plan-your-visit/information-centres

Coniston
Ruskin Avenue
tel 015394 41533

Ambleside
Central Buildings, Market Cross
tel 015394 68135

Walking holidays
Mickledore
www.mickledore.co.uk

Absolute Escapes
www.absoluteescapes.com

Wandering Aengus
www.wanderingængustreks.com

Baggage transfer
Brigantes
www.brigantesenglishwalks.com/
baggage-transfers

Trail Magic Baggage
www.trailmagicbaggage.
com/#Uk_Transfers

Herdwick Travel
https://herdwicktravel.co.uk/
luggage-and-bicycle-transfers/

General accommodation websites
Youth Hostels Association
www.yha.org.uk

Lake District National Park
www.lakedistrict.gov.uk/visiting/
where-to-stay

Visit Cumbria
www.visitcumbria.com/accommodation

National Trust campsites and B&Bs
www.nationaltrust.org.uk/holidays

Campsites
www.ukcampsite.co.uk

Lakeland Camping Barns
www.lakelandcampingbarns.co.uk

Bed and Breakfast
www.bedandbreakfasts.co.uk

Booking.com
www.booking.com

Individual tourist information centres will often be able to help with accommodation in their specific area.

Transport
General information and links to further transport websites
www.visitlakedistrict.com/explore/travel

Buses
www.stagecoachbus.com/about/cumbria-and-north-lancashire

Trains
www.thetrainline.com

Lake launches
for Derwent Water
https://keswick-launch.co.uk
for Windermere
www.windermere-lakecruises.co.uk

Taxis

Ambleside, Grasmere, Langdale, Patterdale
Ambleside Hilltop Taxis
tel 07979 664472

Ambleside Amber Taxis
tel 015394 42000

Eskdale
Sim's Travel
tel 019467 23227

Keswick and Borrowdale
Davies Taxis
tel 017687 72676

Apps
There are apps for Stagecoach Bus, and The Train Line. For general transport planning, Rome2rio is a good choice.

Navigation apps
There are many very good apps available for positioning yourself and navigating using a smartphone. These should always be used in conjunction with a paper map and compass, as phones can run out of battery or have technical issues. Good apps using OS mapping include:

OS Maps
ViewRanger
Memory-Map
Topo GPS
OutDoors GPS

Using a GPS device
You may own and want to use a specific GPS device of your choice. GPS tracks are available for the Tour of the Lake District and can be downloaded from the Cicerone website: www.cicerone.co.uk/1049/GPX.

Weather forecasts

Websites

Lake District National Park
www.lakedistrictweatherline.co.uk

The UK Met Office, Lake District
mountain weather
www.metoffice.gov.uk

Mountain Weather Information Service
www.mwis.org.uk

Apps

Mountain Weather UK
WeatherPro
Met Office

Other useful resources

www.lakesworldheritage.co.uk
www.lakedistrict.gov.uk
www.visitcumbria.com
www.nationaltrust.org.uk

APPENDIX B
Accommodation

The following budget options, listed in route order, are for camping, hostels and bunk-houses at or near the end of each stage, as well as a small selection of other useful accommodation specifically mentioned – although this list is by no means exhaustive. Plentiful accommodation can be found in Ambleside, Coniston, Keswick, Grasmere and Windermere. Smaller communities such as Eskdale, Wasdale, Buttermere, Borrowdale (for Rosthwaite) and Patterdale have fewer options.

See Appendix A for general accommodation websites which will help you identify all other options.

Windermere
YHA Windermere
tel 0345 371 9352

Ambleside
YHA Ambleside
tel 0345 371 9620
www.yha.org.uk

Low Wray Campsite (4km from Ambleside)
tel 015394 32733
www.nationaltrust.org.uk

Skelwith Bridge
Skelwith Bridge Hotel
tel 015394 32115
www.skelwithbridgehotel.co.uk

Elterwater
Elterwater Hostel
tel 01539 437245
www.elterwaterhostel.co.uk

Langdale YHA Langdale (High Close, 1km off route from Elterwater)
tel 0345 371 9748
www.yha.org.uk

Britannia Inn
tel 015394 37210
www.thebritanniainn.com

Baysbrown Farm Campsite
(Chapel Stile, 1km from Elterwater)
tel 015394 37150
www.baysbrownfarmcampsite.co.uk

Coniston
Coniston Hall Campsite
tel 01539 441223
http://conistonhallcampsite.co.uk

YHA Coniston Holly How
tel 0345 371 9511
www.yha.org.uk

The Crown Inn
tel 015394 41243
www.crowninnconiston.com

The Black Bull Inn and Hotel
tel 015394 41335
www.blackbullconiston.co.uk

Shepherds Bridge B&B
tel 015394 41475
www.shepherdsbridgeconiston.com

YHA Coniston Coppermines
tel 0345 371 9630
www.yha.org.uk

Coniston Hoathwaite Campsite (Torver, 3km south of Coniston)
tel 015394 32733
www.nationaltrust.org.uk

Seathwaite

Turner Hall Farm Campsite
tel 01229 716420

Seathwaite Apartments (at Newfield Inn
– two-night stays for 2 or 4 people)
tel 01229 716208
gailseathwaite@gmail.com

High Wallabarrow Camping Barn
tel 01229 715011
www.wallabarrow.co.uk

Eskdale

Eskdale YHA Eskdale
tel 0345 371 9317
www.yha.org.uk

Woolpack Inn
tel 019467 23230
www.woolpack.co.uk

Wha House Farm B&B
tel 019467 23322
www.whahousefarm.co.uk

Eskdale Campsite
tel 015394 32733
www.nationaltrust.org.uk

The Boot Inn
tel 019467 23711
www.thebooteskdale.co.uk

Fisherground Campsite
tel 019467 23723
www.fishergroundcampsite.co.uk

Nether Wasdale

Church Stile Farm and Holiday Park
tel 019467 26252
www.churchstile.co.uk

Strands Hotel/Screes Inn
tel 019467 26237
www.strands-brewery.co.uk

Wasdale

Wasdale National Trust Campsite
tel 015394 32733

Wasdale Head Inn
tel 019467 26229
www.wasdale.com
Small campsite opposite the inn (small
tents only, no bookings)also for booking
B&B at Lingmell House Farm

Burnthwaite Farm B&B
tel 019467 26242
www.burnthwaite.co.uk

YHA Black Sail
tel 0345 371 9680
www.yha.org.uk

Buttermere

YHA Buttermere
tel 0345 371 9508
www.yha.org.uk

Syke Farm Campsite
tel 017687 70222
www.sykefarmcampsite.com

Buttermere Court Hotel (The Fish Inn)
tel 017687 70253
https://buttermerecourthotel.co.uk

The Bridge Hotel
tel 017687 70252
www.bridge-hotel.com

Cragg House Farm Camping Barn
tel 017687 70204
www.lakelandcampingbarns.co.uk

Keswick

YHA Keswick
tel 0345 371 9746
www.yha.org.uk

Denton House Hostel
tel 017687 75351
www.dentonhouse-keswick.co.uk

Keswick Camping and Caravanning Club site, Crow Park
tel 017687 72392

Derwentwater Camping and Caravanning Club site
tel 017687 72579
www.campingandcaravanningclub.co.uk

Castlerigg Hall Camping
tel 017687 74499
www.castlerigg.co.uk

Rosthwaite
YHA Borrowdale (at Longthwaite, 500 metres from Rosthwaite)
tel 0345 371 9624
www.yha.org.uk

Chapel House Farm Campsite
tel 017687 77256
www.chapelhousefarmcampsite.co.uk

Royal Oak Hotel
tel 017687 77214
www.royaloakhotel.co.uk

Yew Tree Farm Guest House
tel 017687 77675
www.borrowdaleyewtreefarm.co.uk

Stonethwaite Farm Camping Site
tel 017687 77234
www.stonethwaitefarm.co.uk

Grasmere
YHA Grasmere Butharlyp Howe
tel 0345 371 9319
www.yha.org.uk

Thorney Howe Hostel and Bunkhouse
tel 01539 435 597
www.thorneyhow.co.uk

Rydal Hall Campsite and Bunkhouse (approximately 2km from Grasmere and Ambleside)
tel 01539 432050
https://rydalhall.org

Patterdale
Gillside Camping and Caravan Park (at Glenridding, 1.5km)
tel 017684 82346
www.gillsidecaravanandcampingsite.co.uk

YHA Patterdale
tel 0345 371 9337
www.yha.org.uk

White Lion Inn
tel 017684 82214
www.whitelionpatterdale.com

Old Water View B&B
tel 017684 82175
www.oldwaterview.co.uk

Crookey Cottage B&B
tel 017684 82278
www.crookeycottage.com

Side Farm Camping
tel 017684 82337
www.lakedistrictcamping.co.uk/campsite_side_farm.php

Sykeside Camping Park/Brotherswater Inn (approx 500 metres off route)
tel 01768 482239
https://sykeside.co.uk

APPENDIX C

Facilities table

Location	Distance from start (km)	Distance from previous location (low-level route)	Distance from previous location (high-level route)	Tourist info	Hotel/ B&B	Campsite	Hostel/ Barn	Café/ Restaurant	Pub	Shop	Bank/ ATM	Transport
Windermere				X	X	X	X	X	X	X	X	555 bus, lake ferry
Ambleside	6.2	10.5	10.5	X	X	X	X	X	X	X	X	516 bus
Skelwith Bridge		6.2	6.2		X			X	X	X		516 bus
Elterwater	8.8	2.6	2.6		X	>1km	<1km	X	X	<1km		516 bus
Little Langdale	11	2	2		X				X			
Coniston	20	9.2	9.2	X	X	X	X	X	X	X	X	505 bus
Seathwaite	29	9	11			<1km	>1km		X			
Eskdale (Doctor Bridge)	38	9	12		X	X	<0.5km	X	X			La'al Ratty railway
Eskdale Green	43.5	5.5			X	X	X	X	X	X		
Nether Wasdale (off route)	48.5	5			X	X	<2km	X	X	X		

Location	Distance from start (km)	Distance from previous location (low-level route)	Distance from previous location (high-level route)	Tourist info	Hotel/B&B	Campsite	Hostel/Barn	Café/Restaurant	Pub	Shop	Bank/ATM	Transport
Wasdale Head	56	9.5	17		X	X			X	X		
Black Sail Youth Hostel	62	6					X					
Buttermere	68	6	16.5		X	X	X	X	X			77/77A bus (seasonal)
Rowling End Farm	78	10	11		>1km		<1km					
Portinscale	82	4	4		X	X	X	X	X	X		
Keswick	84	2	2	X	X	X	X	X	X	X	X	555, 78, X4 and X5 buses, Keswick launch
Ashness Bridge	92.5	8.5	8.5		<1km							78 bus, Keswick launch
Rosthwaite	99.5	7	7		X	X	>1km	X	X			78 bus
Grasmere	113.5	14	14	X	X	X	X	X	X	X	X	555 bus
Grisedale Tarn	117	6	6									

Location	Distance from start (km)	Distance from previous location (low-level route)	Distance from previous location (high-level route)	Tourist info	Hotel/ B&B	Campsite	Hostel/ Barn	Café/ Restaurant	Pub	Shop	Bank/ ATM	Transport
Patterdale	126.5	7	10		X	>1km	X	X	X	X	X	
Scandale Pass	135.5	9	9									
Ambleside	144.5	6	9	X	X	X	X	X	X	X	X	

For bus, train and ferry routes, see the transport map in the Introduction, and see Appendix A for the company websites, where timetables are available.

APPENDIX D

Place names

Local place names and meanings encountered on the Tour, but not explained within the main text

Name	Meaning
Ambleside	Old Norse 'The Shieling on the sandbank by the river'
Ashness	Old Norse 'The promontory where ash trees grow'
Black Sail	Old English and Old Norse 'The dark stream or bog'
Buttermere	Old English 'The lake with rich butter pastures'
Causey Pike	Old and Middle English, and Old Norse 'The peak by the causeway'
Coniston	Old Norse 'The king's manor'
Great Gable and Green Gable	Old Norse 'The mountain shaped like the gable of a house/ the grassy hill shaped like a gable'
Greenup Gill	Old English and Old Norse 'The stream in the ravine in the green secluded valley'
Keswick	Old English 'The cheese or dairy farm'
Langdale	Old Norse 'The long valley' (as opposed to Scandale, meaning 'The short valley')
Mickledore	Old Norse and Old English 'The great gap'
Moses' Trod	A quarryman at Honister allegedly used this path to smuggle illegally distilled whisky and graphite in exchange for tobacco and rum from Ravenglass
Orrest Head	Old Norse and Middle English 'The site of a battle'
Sail	Old Norse 'The marshy mountain'

Name	Meaning
Scafell	Old Norse 'The peak of the bare, stony mountain'
Scarth Gap Pass	Old Norse 'The pass over the col'
Sweden Bridge	Old Norse 'The bridge on the land cleared by burning'
Tarn Hows	Old Norse 'The tarn among the hills'

Place-name elements

Word	Meaning
Beck, gill, ghyll	Old Norse for a stream
Fell	hill or mountain
Garth	enclosure
Hause	mountain pass
How	hill
Keld	spring
Knott	rocky hilltop
Mere	lake
Moss	bog
Pike	peak
Thwaite	Old Norse for a clearing

APPENDIX E
Further reading and resources

Lake District Place Names by Robert Gambles, Hayloft Publishing, 2013

The Buildings of Cumbria by Matthew Hyde and Nikolaus Pevsner, Yale University Press, 2014

The Cumbrian Dictionary of Dialect, Tradition and Folklore by William Rollinson, Smith Settle, 1997

Rocks and Rain, Reason and Romance by David Howe, Saraband, 2019

The AA guide to the Lake District and Cumbria, AA Publishing, 3rd edition, 2018

Traditional Buildings of Cumbria by RW Brunskill, Cassell, 2002

Navigation Mini-Guide by Pete Hawkins, Cicerone, 2nd edition, 2019

Map and Compass by Pete Hawkins, Cicerone, 2nd edition, 2019

DOWNLOAD THE ROUTES IN GPX FORMAT

All the routes in this guide are available for download from:

www.cicerone.co.uk/1049/GPX

as GPX files. You should be able to load them into most formats of mobile device, whether GPS or smartphone.

When you go to this link, you will be asked for your email address and where you purchased the guide, and have the option to subscribe to the Cicerone e-newsletter.

www.cicerone.co.uk

LISTING OF CICERONE GUIDES

BRITISH ISLES CHALLENGES, COLLECTIONS AND ACTIVITIES

Cycling Land's End to John o' Groats
The Big Rounds
The Book of the Bothy
The C2C Cycle Route
The End to End Cycle Route
The Mountains of England and Wales: Vol 1 Wales
The Mountains of England and Wales: Vol 2 England
The National Trails
Walking The End to End Trail

SCOTLAND

Backpacker's Britain: Northern Scotland
Ben Nevis and Glen Coe
Cycle Touring in Northern Scotland
Cycling in the Hebrides
Great Mountain Days in Scotland
Mountain Biking in Southern and Central Scotland
Mountain Biking in West and North West Scotland
Not the West Highland Way Scotland
Scotland's Best Small Mountains
Scotland's Mountain Ridges
Skye's Cuillin Ridge Traverse
The Ayrshire and Arran Coastal Paths
The Borders Abbeys Way
The Great Glen Way
The Great Glen Way Map Booklet
The Hebridean Way
The Hebrides
The Isle of Mull
The Isle of Skye
The Skye Trail
The Southern Upland Way
The Speyside Way
The Speyside Way Map Booklet
The West Highland Way
The West Highland Way Map Booklet
Walking Highland Perthshire
Walking in the Cairngorms
Walking in the Pentland Hills
Walking in the Scottish Borders
Walking in the Southern Uplands
Walking in Torridon
Walking Loch Lomond and the Trossachs
Walking on Arran
Walking on Harris and Lewis
Walking on Jura, Islay and Colonsay
Walking on Rum and the Small Isles
Walking on the Orkney and Shetland Isles
Walking on Uist and Barra
Walking the Cape Wrath Trail

Walking the Corbetts
Vol 1 South of the Great Glen
Vol 2 North of the Great Glen
Walking the Galloway Hills
Walking the Munros
Vol 1 – Southern, Central and Western Highlands
Vol 2 – Northern Highlands and the Cairngorms
Winter Climbs Ben Nevis and Glen Coe
Winter Climbs in the Cairngorms

NORTHERN ENGLAND TRAILS

Hadrian's Wall Path
Hadrian's Wall Path Map Booklet
The Coast to Coast Walk
The Coast to Coast Walk Map Booklet
The Dales Way
The Dales Way Map Booklet
The Pennine Way
The Pennine Way Map Booklet
Walking the Tour of the Lake District

NORTH EAST ENGLAND, YORKSHIRE DALES AND PENNINES

Cycling in the Yorkshire Dales
Great Mountain Days in the Pennines
Mountain Biking in the Yorkshire Dales
St Oswald's Way and St Cuthbert's Way
The Cleveland Way and the Yorkshire Wolds Way
The Cleveland Way Map Booklet
The North York Moors
The Reivers Way
The Teesdale Way
Trail and Fell Running in the Yorkshire Dales
Walking in County Durham
Walking in Northumberland
Walking in the North Pennines
Walking in the Yorkshire Dales: North and East
Walking in the Yorkshire Dales: South and West

NORTH WEST ENGLAND THE ISLE OF MAN

Cycling the Pennine Bridleway
Cycling the Way of the Roses
Hadrian's Cycleway
Isle of Man Coastal Path
The Lancashire Cycleway
The Lune Valley and Howgills
Walking in Cumbria's Eden Valley
Walking in Lancashire

Walking in the Forest of Bowland and Pendle
Walking on the Isle of Man
Walking on the West Pennine Moors
Walks in Silverdale and Arnside

LAKE DISTRICT

Cycling in the Lake District
Great Mountain Days in the Lake District
Lake District Winter Climbs
Lake District: High Level and Fell Walks
Lake District: Low Level and Lake Walks
Mountain Biking in the Lake District
Outdoor Adventures with Children – Lake District
Scrambles in the Lake District – North
Scrambles in the Lake District – South
The Cumbria Way
Trail and Fell Running in the Lake District
Walking the Lake District Fells:
Borrowdale
Buttermere
Coniston
Keswick
Langdale
Mardale and the Far East
Patterdale
Wasdale

DERBYSHIRE, PEAK DISTRICT AND MIDLANDS

Cycling in the Peak District
Dark Peak Walks
Scrambles in the Dark Peak
Walking in Derbyshire
Walking in the Peak District – White Peak East

SOUTHERN ENGLAND

20 Classic Sportive Rides in South East England
20 Classic Sportive Rides in South West England
Cycling in the Cotswolds
Mountain Biking on the North Downs
Mountain Biking on the South Downs
Suffolk Coast and Heath Walks
The Cotswold Way
The Cotswold Way Map Booklet
The Great Stones Way
The Kennet and Avon Canal
The Lea Valley Walk
The North Downs Way
The North Downs Way Map Booklet

For full information on all our guides,
books and eBooks,
visit our website:
www.cicerone.co.uk